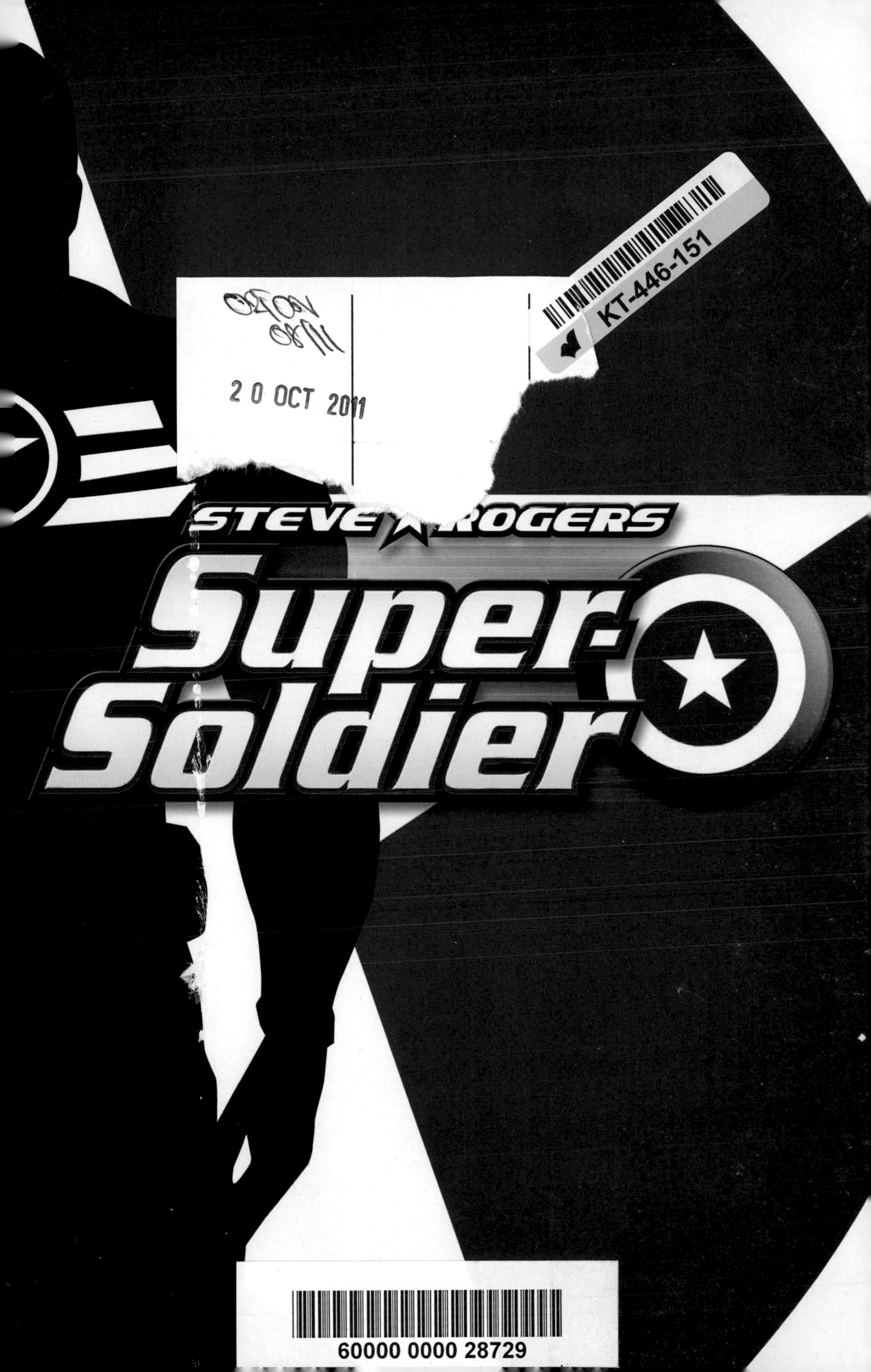
STEVE ROGERS
Super-Soldier

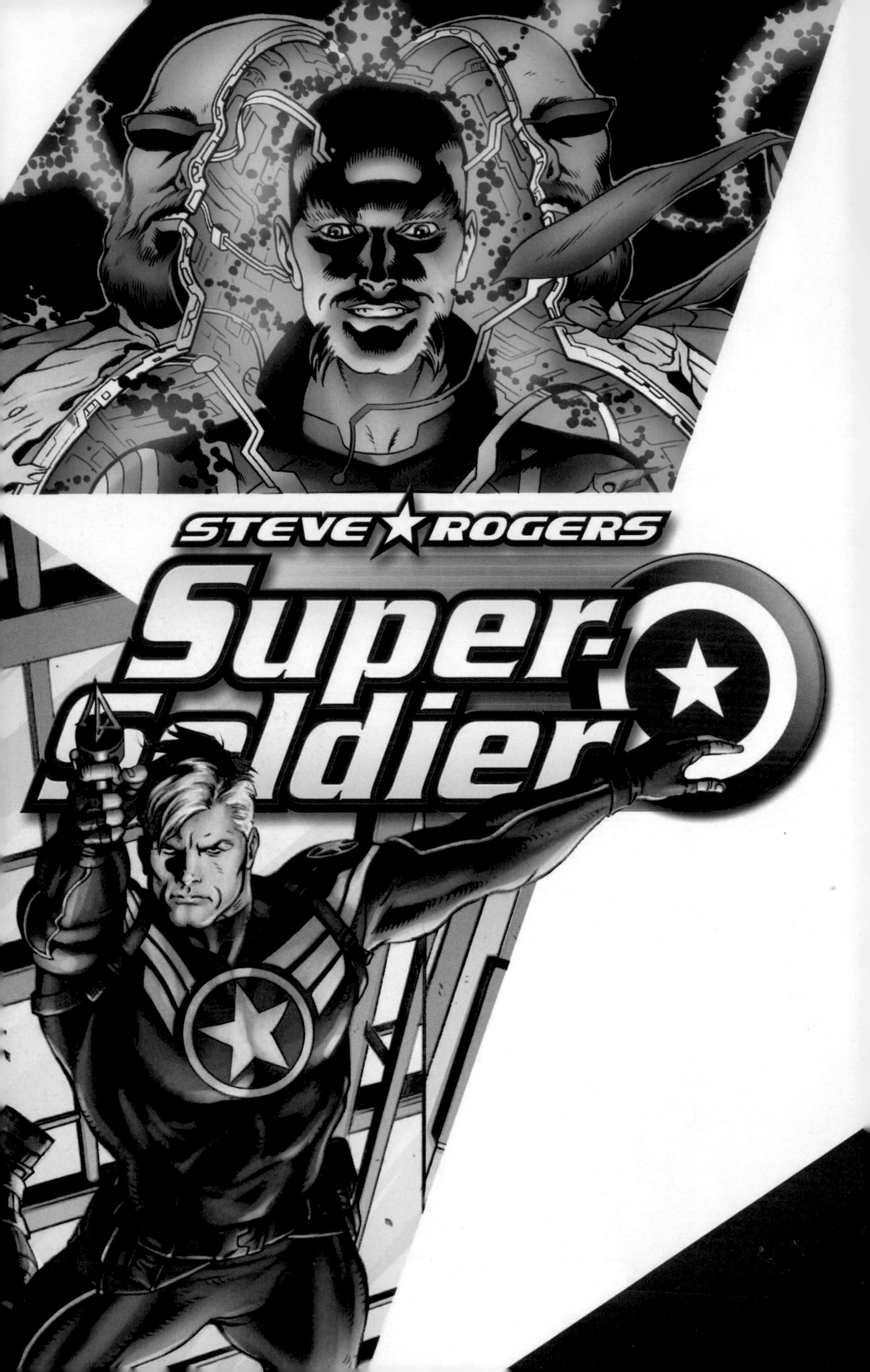
STEVE ROGERS
Super-Soldier

Writer
ED BRUBAKER
Artist
DALE EAGLESHAM

Letterer: **VC'S JOE CARAMAGNA**

Cover Art: **CARLOS PACHECO, TIM TOWNSEND & FRANK D'ARMATA**

Associate Editor: **LAUREN SANKOVITCH**

Editor: **TOM BREVOORT**

Captain America created by **JOE SIMON** & **JACK KIRBY**

Collection Editor: **JENNIFER GRÜNWALD**

Editorial Assistants: **JAMES EMMETT & JOE HOCHSTEIN**

Assistant Editors: **ALEX STARBUCK** & **NELSON RIBEIRO**

Editor, Special Projects: **MARK D. BEAZLEY**

Senior Editor, Special Projects: **JEFF YOUNGQUIST**

Senior Vice President of Sales: **DAVID GABRIEL**

SVP of Brand Planning & Communications: **MICHAEL PASCIULLO**

Book Designer: **RODOLFO MURAGUCHI**

Editor in Chief: **AXEL ALONSO**

Chief Creative Officer: **JOE QUESADA**

Publisher: **DAN BUCKLEY**

Executive Producer: **ALAN FINE**

STEVE ROGERS: SUPER-SOLDIER. Contains material originally published in magazine form as STEVE ... ...4879-1. Published by MARVEL WORLDWIDE, INC., a subsidiary of MARVEL ENTERTAINMENT, L... ...arvel Characters, Inc. All rights reserved. $14.99 per copy in the U.S. and $16.50 in Canada (... ...and likenesses thereof, and all related indicia are trademarks of Marvel Characters, Inc... ...g or dead person or institution is intended, and any such similarity which may exis... ...CMO Marvel Characters B.V.; DAN BUCKLEY, Publisher & President - Print, Animat... ...Business Affairs & Talent Management; TOM BREVOORT, SVP of Publishing; C.B... ...VP of Brand Planning & Communications; JIM O'KEEFE, VP of Operations &... ...GAN CRESPI, Editorial Operations Manager; ALEX MORALES, Publishing... ...contact John Dokes, SVP Integrated Sales and Marketing, at jdokes... ...NNELLEY, INC., SALEM, VA, USA.

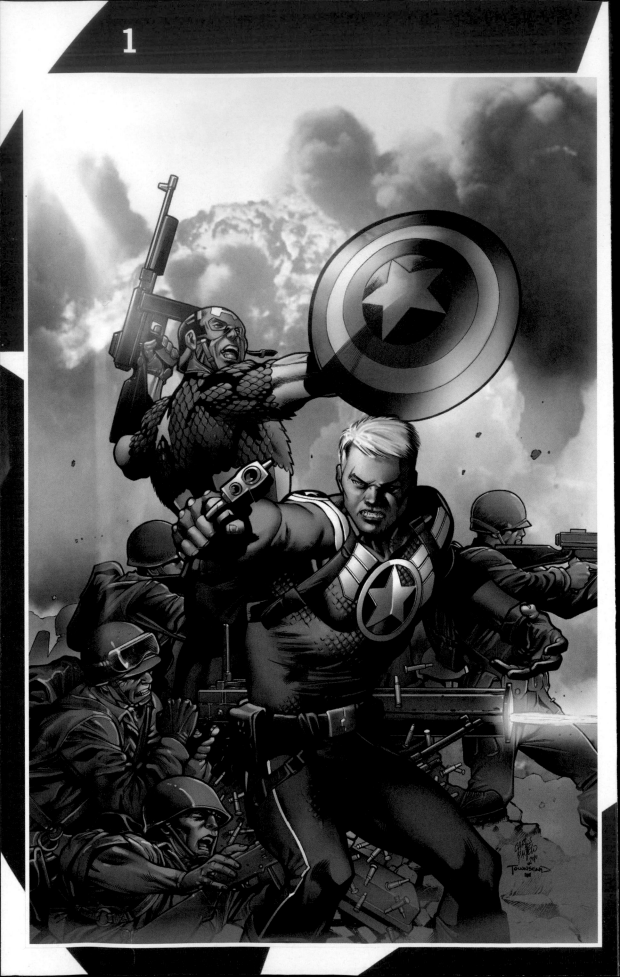

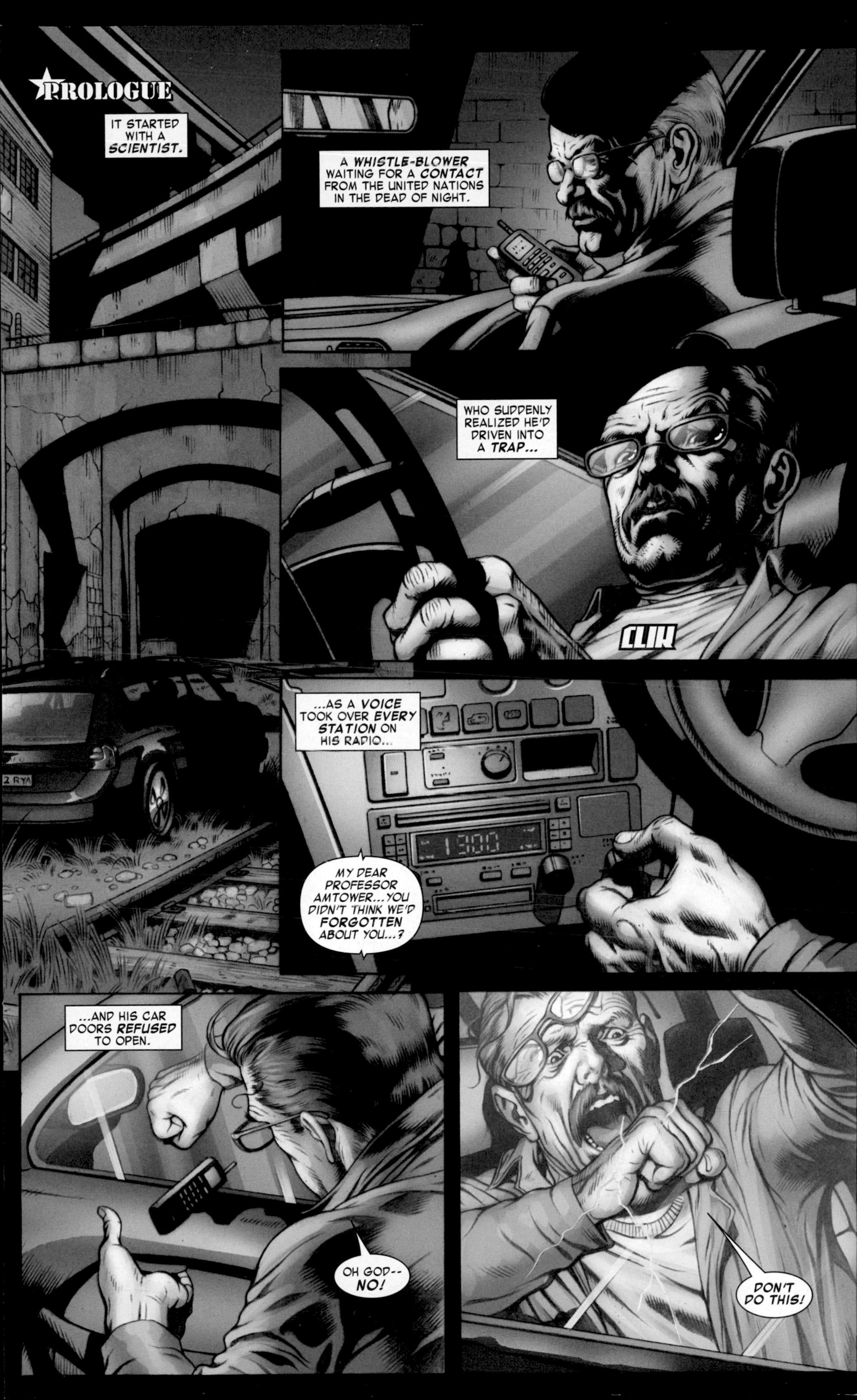
PROLOGUE
IT STARTED WITH A SCIENTIST.
A WHISTLE-BLOWER WAITING FOR A CONTACT FROM THE UNITED NATIONS IN THE DEAD OF NIGHT.
WHO SUDDENLY REALIZED HE'D DRIVEN INTO A TRAP...
CLIK
...AS A VOICE TOOK OVER EVERY STATION ON HIS RADIO...
MY DEAR PROFESSOR AMTOWER... YOU DIDN'T THINK WE'D FORGOTTEN ABOUT YOU...?
...AND HIS CAR DOORS REFUSED TO OPEN.
OH GOD-- NO!
DON'T DO THIS!

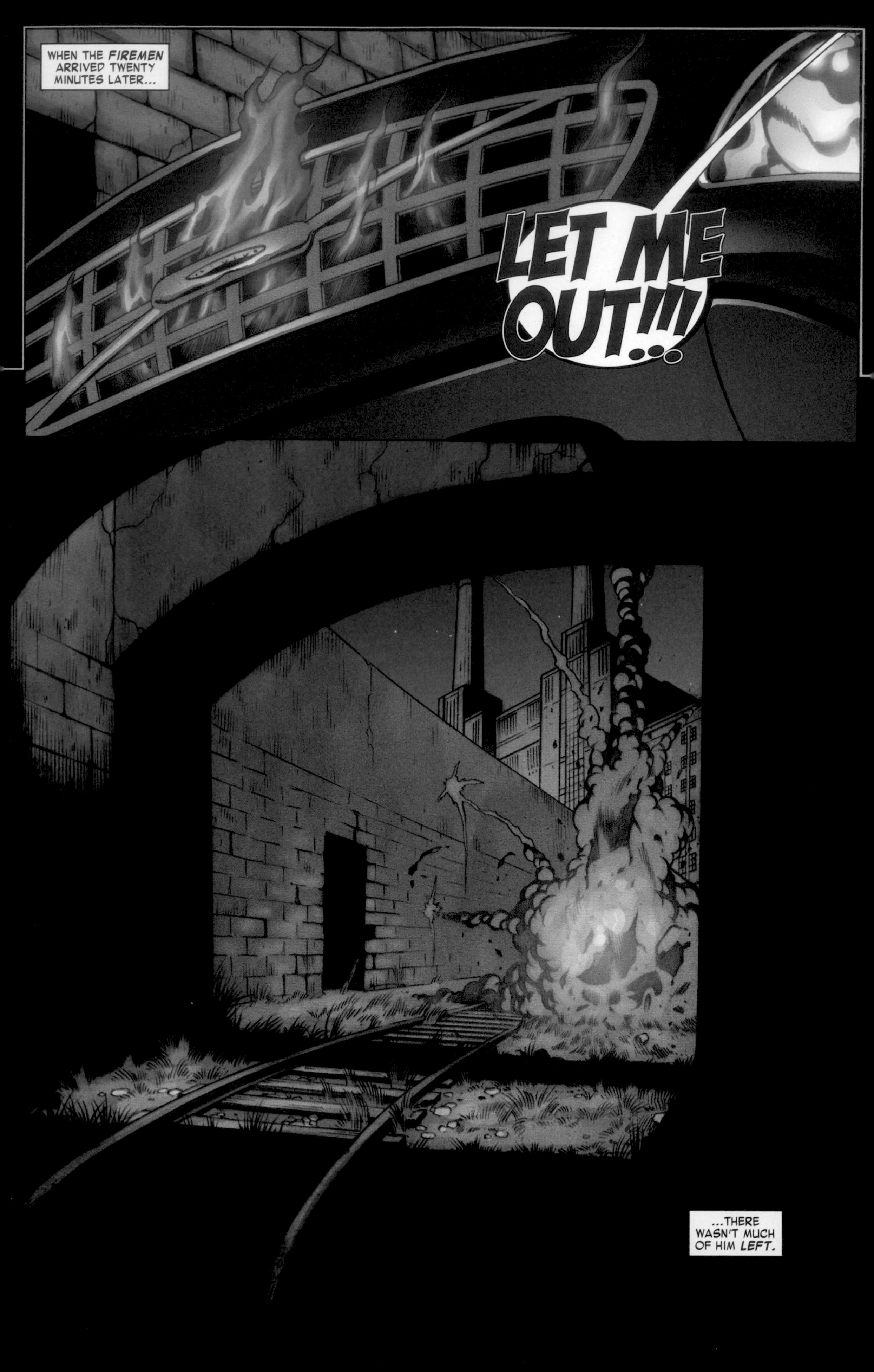
WHEN THE FIREMEN ARRIVED TWENTY MINUTES LATER...
LET ME OUT!!!
...THERE WASN'T MUCH OF HIM LEFT.

1

IN THE DARK DAYS OF THE EARLY 1940s,
STEVE ROGERS,
A STRUGGLING YOUNG ARTIST FROM THE
LOWER EAST SIDE OF MANHATTAN,
FOUND HIMSELF HORRIFIED BY THE WAR RAGING OVERSEAS.
DESPERATE TO HELP, HE WAS REJECTED BY THE
U.S. ARMY
AS UNFIT FOR SERVICE WHEN HE TRIED TO ENLIST.

UNDETERRED, CONVINCED THIS WAS WHERE HE NEEDED TO BE,
HE WAS SELECTED TO PARTICIPATE IN
A COVERT MILITARY PROJECT CALLED
OPERATION: REBIRTH.
THERE, HE WAS CHOSEN BY SCIENTIST ABRAHAM ERSKINE
AS THE FIRST HUMAN TEST SUBJECT, AND OVERNIGHT WAS
TRANSFORMED INTO
**AMERICA'S FIRST SUPER-SOLDIER,
CAPTAIN AMERICA.**

NOW, DECADES LATER, STEVE ROGERS CARRIES ON THE
BATTLE FOR FREEDOM AND DEMOCRACY AS
**AMERICA'S TOP
LAW-ENFORCEMENT OPERATIVE
AND COMMANDER OF
THE MIGHTY AVENGERS.**

STEVE ROGERS:
SUPER-SOLDIER

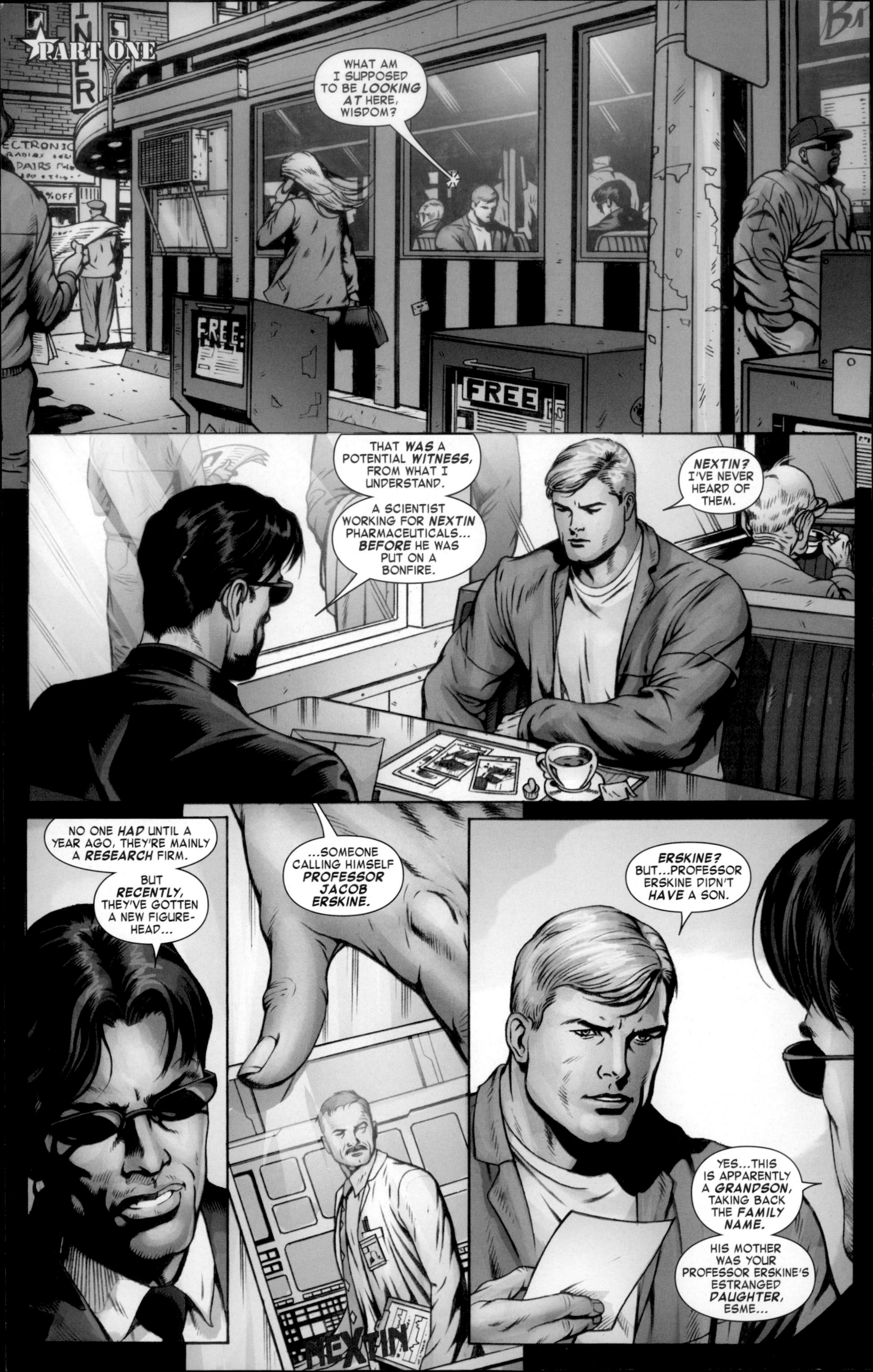
PART ONE
WHAT AM I SUPPOSED TO BE LOOKING AT HERE, WISDOM?
FREE
FREE
THAT WAS A POTENTIAL WITNESS, FROM WHAT I UNDERSTAND.
A SCIENTIST WORKING FOR NEXTIN PHARMACEUTICALS... BEFORE HE WAS PUT ON A BONFIRE.
NEXTIN? I'VE NEVER HEARD OF THEM.
NO ONE HAD UNTIL A YEAR AGO, THEY'RE MAINLY A RESEARCH FIRM.
BUT RECENTLY, THEY'VE GOTTEN A NEW FIGURE-HEAD...
...SOMEONE CALLING HIMSELF PROFESSOR JACOB ERSKINE.
NEXTIN
ERSKINE? BUT...PROFESSOR ERSKINE DIDN'T HAVE A SON.
YES...THIS IS APPARENTLY A GRANDSON, TAKING BACK THE FAMILY NAME.
HIS MOTHER WAS YOUR PROFESSOR ERSKINE'S ESTRANGED DAUGHTER, ESME...

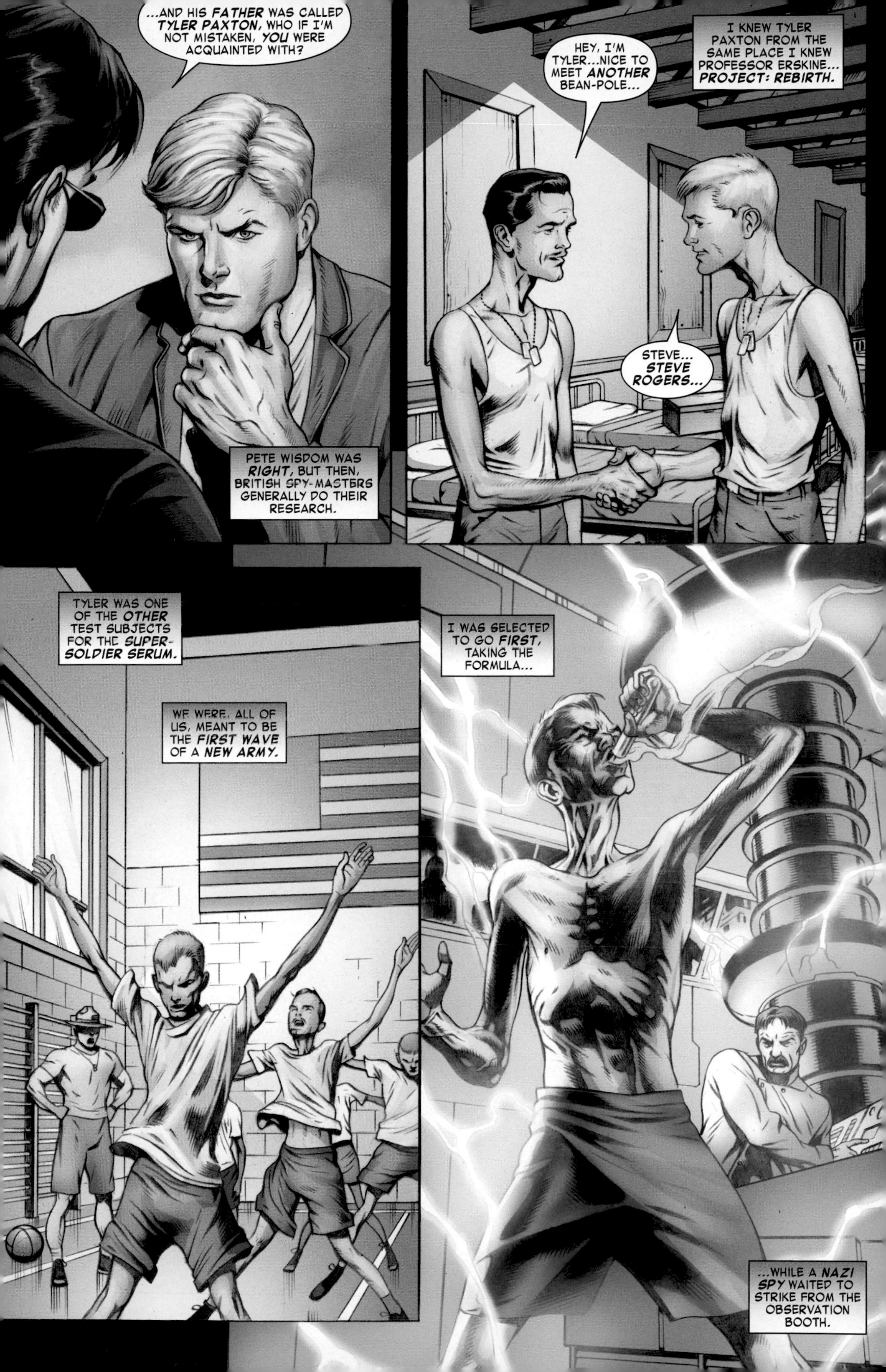
...AND HIS FATHER WAS CALLED TYLER PAXTON, WHO IF I'M NOT MISTAKEN, YOU WERE ACQUAINTED WITH?
PETE WISDOM WAS RIGHT, BUT THEN, BRITISH SPY-MASTERS GENERALLY DO THEIR RESEARCH.
I KNEW TYLER PAXTON FROM THE SAME PLACE I KNEW PROFESSOR ERSKINE... PROJECT: REBIRTH.
HEY, I'M TYLER...NICE TO MEET ANOTHER BEAN-POLE...
STEVE... STEVE ROGERS...
TYLER WAS ONE OF THE OTHER TEST SUBJECTS FOR THE SUPER-SOLDIER SERUM.
WE WERE, ALL OF US, MEANT TO BE THE FIRST WAVE OF A NEW ARMY.
I WAS SELECTED TO GO FIRST, TAKING THE FORMULA...
...WHILE A NAZI SPY WAITED TO STRIKE FROM THE OBSERVATION BOOTH.

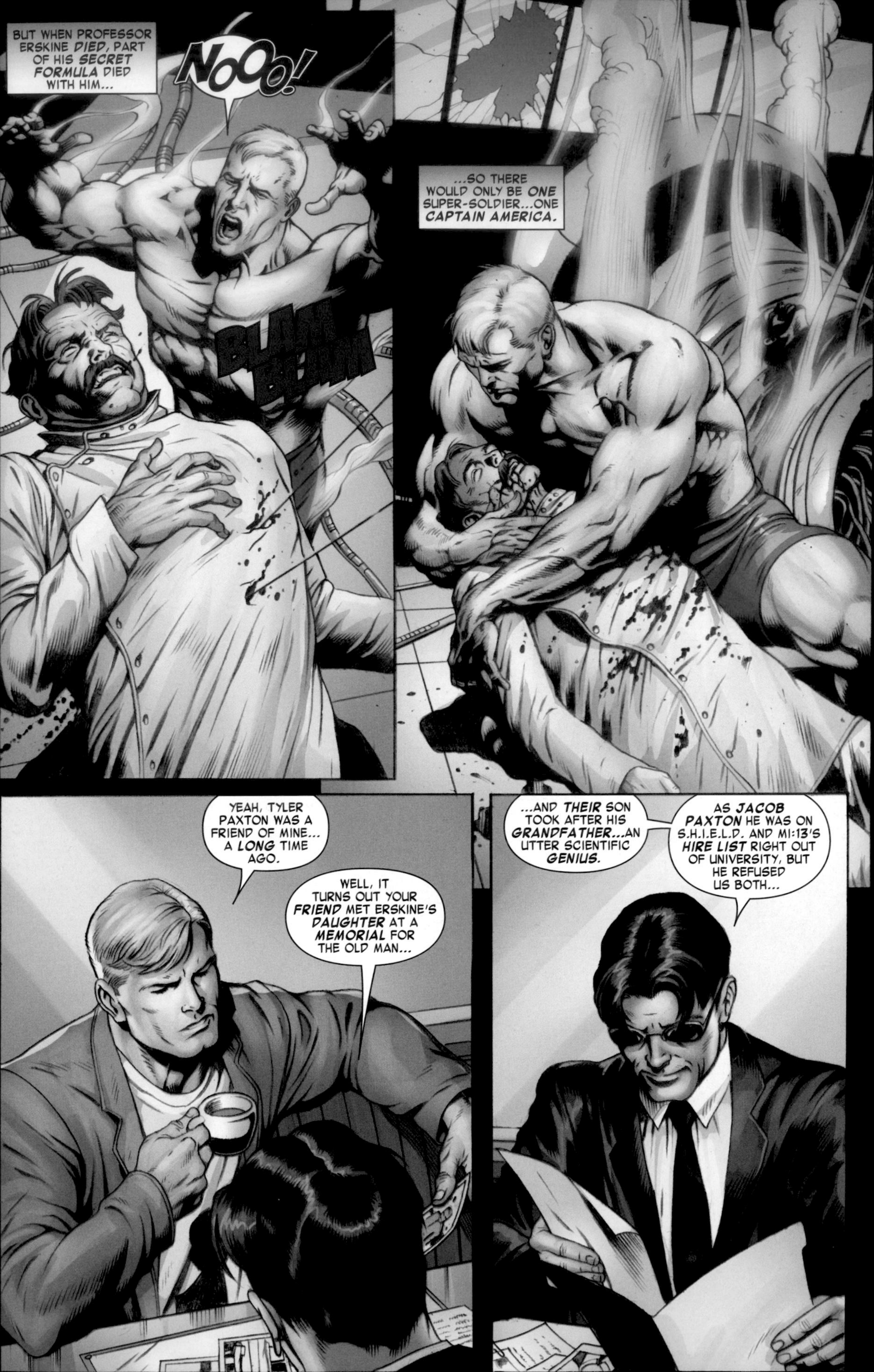
BUT WHEN PROFESSOR ERSKINE *DIED*, PART OF HIS *SECRET FORMULA* DIED WITH HIM...
NOOO!
BLAM BLAM
...SO THERE WOULD ONLY BE *ONE* SUPER-SOLDIER...ONE *CAPTAIN AMERICA.*
YEAH, TYLER PAXTON WAS A FRIEND OF MINE... A *LONG* TIME AGO.
WELL, IT TURNS OUT YOUR *FRIEND* MET ERSKINE'S *DAUGHTER* AT A *MEMORIAL* FOR THE OLD MAN...
...AND *THEIR* SON TOOK AFTER HIS *GRANDFATHER*...AN UTTER SCIENTIFIC *GENIUS.*
AS *JACOB PAXTON* HE WAS ON S.H.I.E.L.D. AND MI:13'S *HIRE LIST* RIGHT OUT OF UNIVERSITY, BUT HE REFUSED US BOTH...

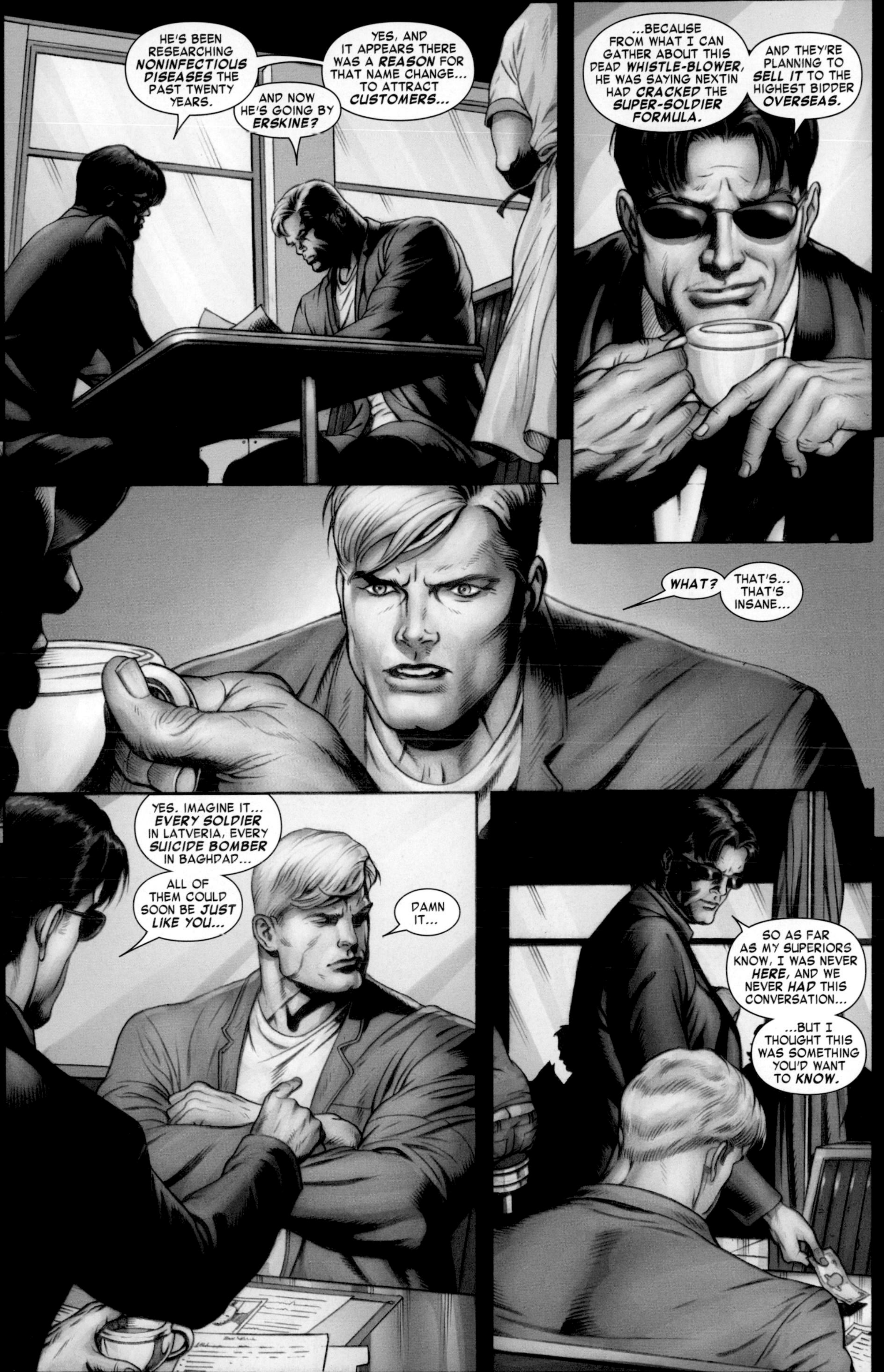
HE'S BEEN RESEARCHING NONINFECTIOUS DISEASES THE PAST TWENTY YEARS.
AND NOW HE'S GOING BY ERSKINE?
YES, AND IT APPEARS THERE WAS A REASON FOR THAT NAME CHANGE... TO ATTRACT CUSTOMERS...
...BECAUSE FROM WHAT I CAN GATHER ABOUT THIS DEAD WHISTLE-BLOWER, HE WAS SAYING NEXTIN HAD CRACKED THE SUPER-SOLDIER FORMULA.
AND THEY'RE PLANNING TO SELL IT TO THE HIGHEST BIDDER OVERSEAS.
WHAT?
THAT'S... THAT'S INSANE...
YES. IMAGINE IT... EVERY SOLDIER IN LATVERIA, EVERY SUICIDE BOMBER IN BAGHDAD...
ALL OF THEM COULD SOON BE JUST LIKE YOU...
DAMN IT...
SO AS FAR AS MY SUPERIORS KNOW, I WAS NEVER HERE, AND WE NEVER HAD THIS CONVERSATION...
...BUT I THOUGHT THIS WAS SOMETHING YOU'D WANT TO KNOW.

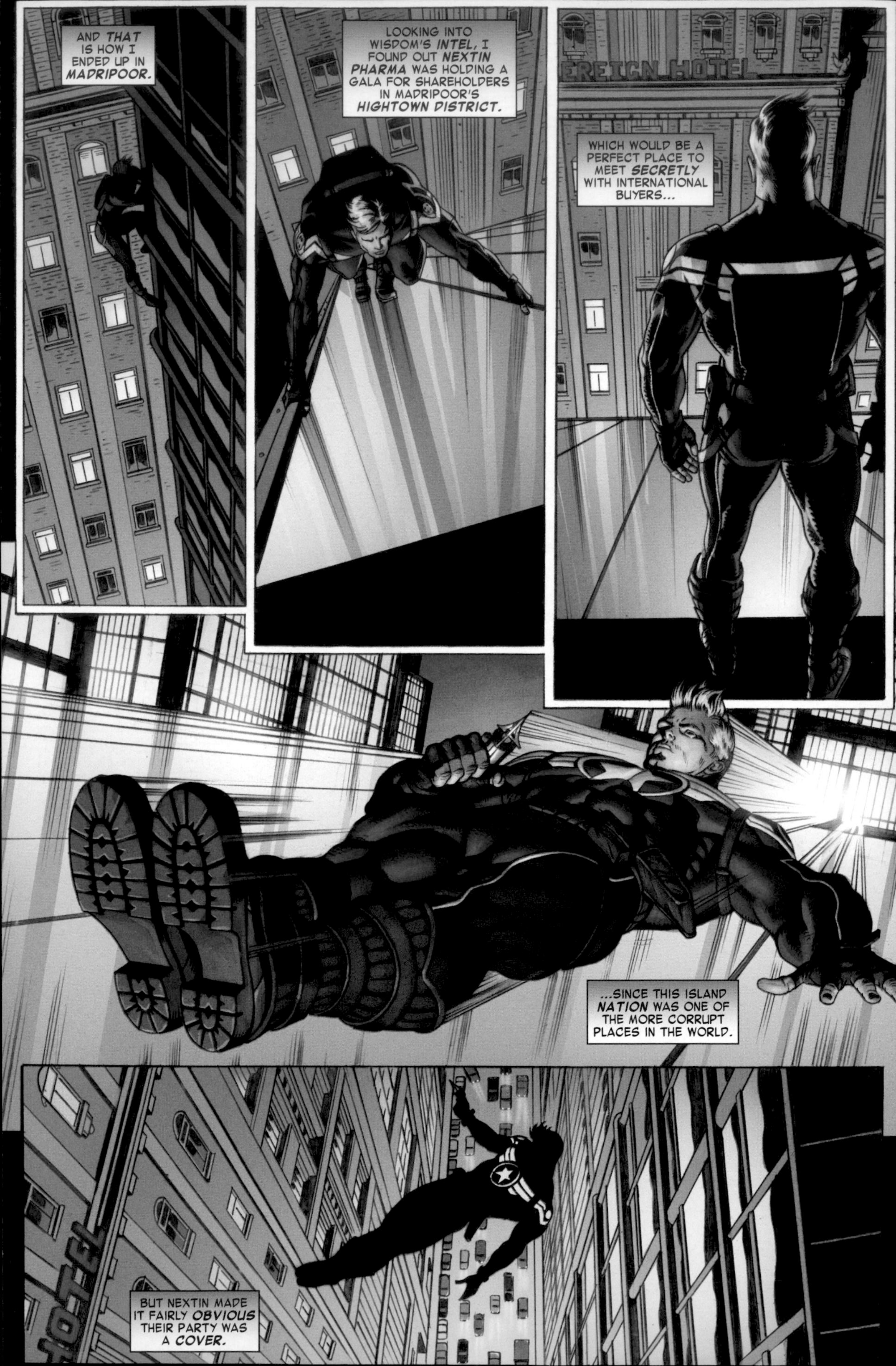
AND THAT IS HOW I ENDED UP IN MADRIPOOR.
LOOKING INTO WISDOM'S INTEL, I FOUND OUT NEXTIN PHARMA WAS HOLDING A GALA FOR SHAREHOLDERS IN MADRIPOOR'S HIGHTOWN DISTRICT.
WHICH WOULD BE A PERFECT PLACE TO MEET SECRETLY WITH INTERNATIONAL BUYERS...
...SINCE THIS ISLAND NATION WAS ONE OF THE MORE CORRUPT PLACES IN THE WORLD.
BUT NEXTIN MADE IT FAIRLY OBVIOUS THEIR PARTY WAS A COVER.

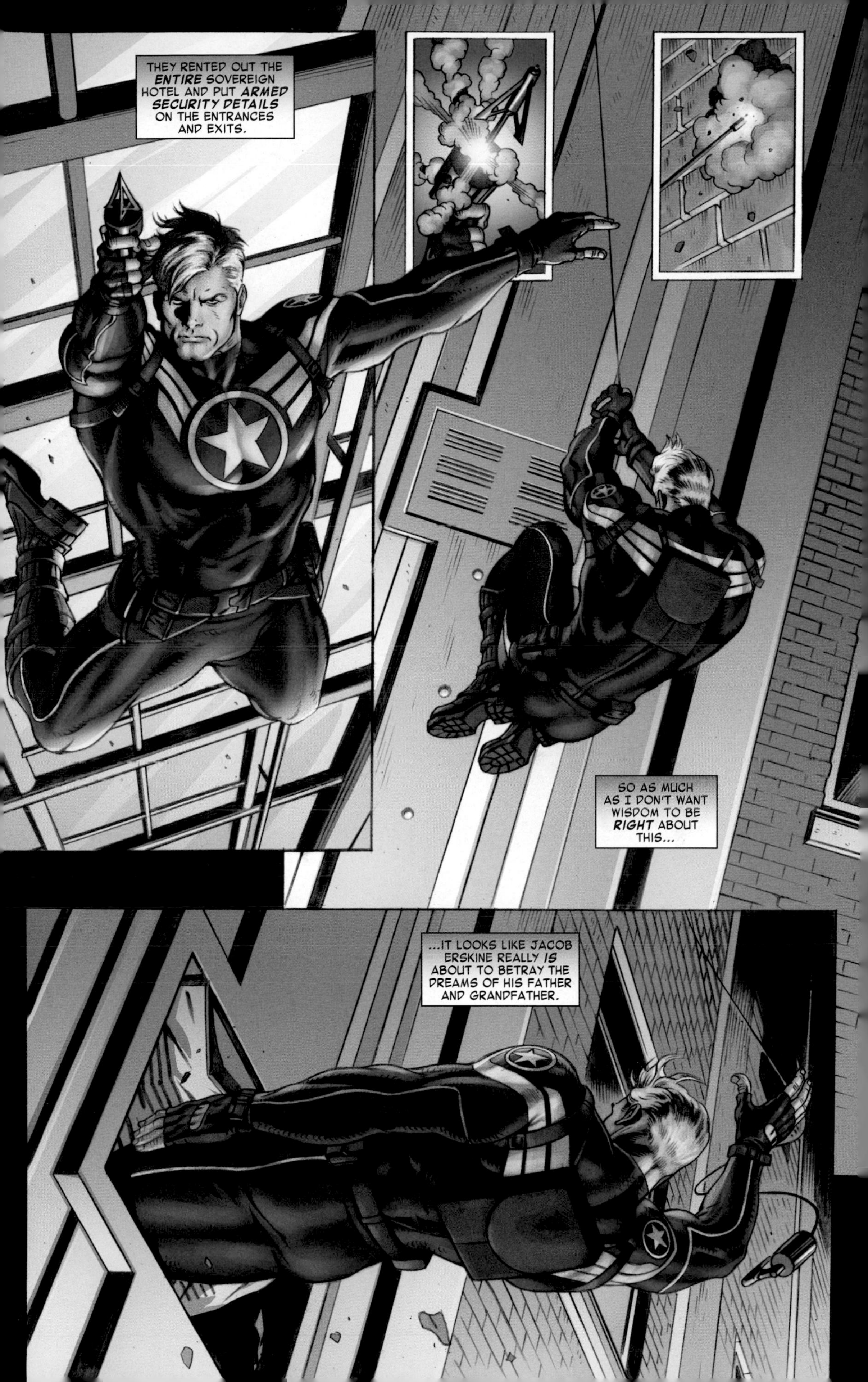
THEY RENTED OUT THE ENTIRE SOVEREIGN HOTEL AND PUT ARMED SECURITY DETAILS ON THE ENTRANCES AND EXITS.
SO AS MUCH AS I DON'T WANT WISDOM TO BE RIGHT ABOUT THIS...
...IT LOOKS LIKE JACOB ERSKINE REALLY IS ABOUT TO BETRAY THE DREAMS OF HIS FATHER AND GRANDFATHER.

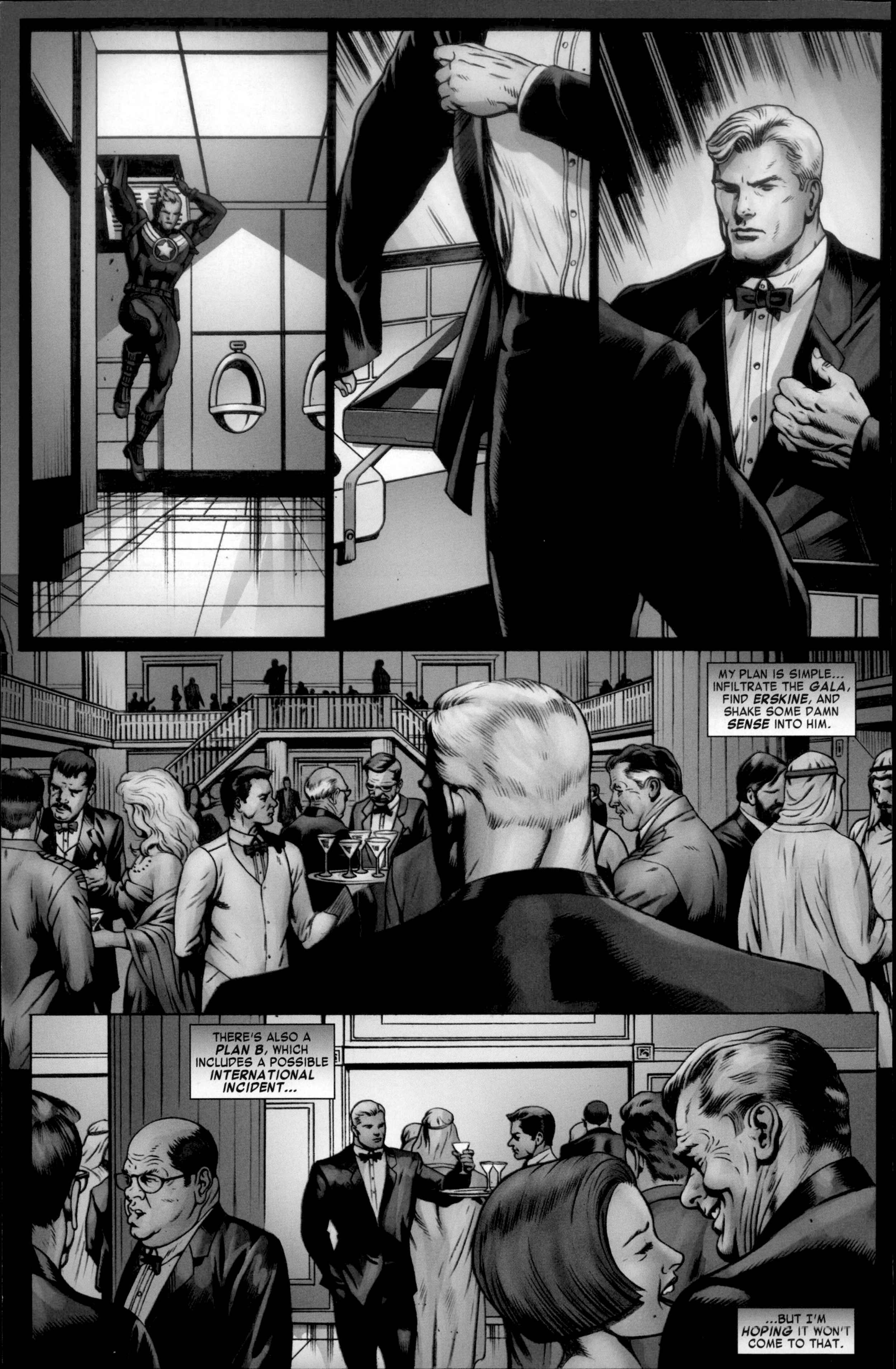
MY PLAN IS SIMPLE... INFILTRATE THE GALA, FIND ERSKINE, AND SHAKE SOME DAMN SENSE INTO HIM.
THERE'S ALSO A PLAN B, WHICH INCLUDES A POSSIBLE INTERNATIONAL INCIDENT...
...BUT I'M HOPING IT WON'T COME TO THAT.

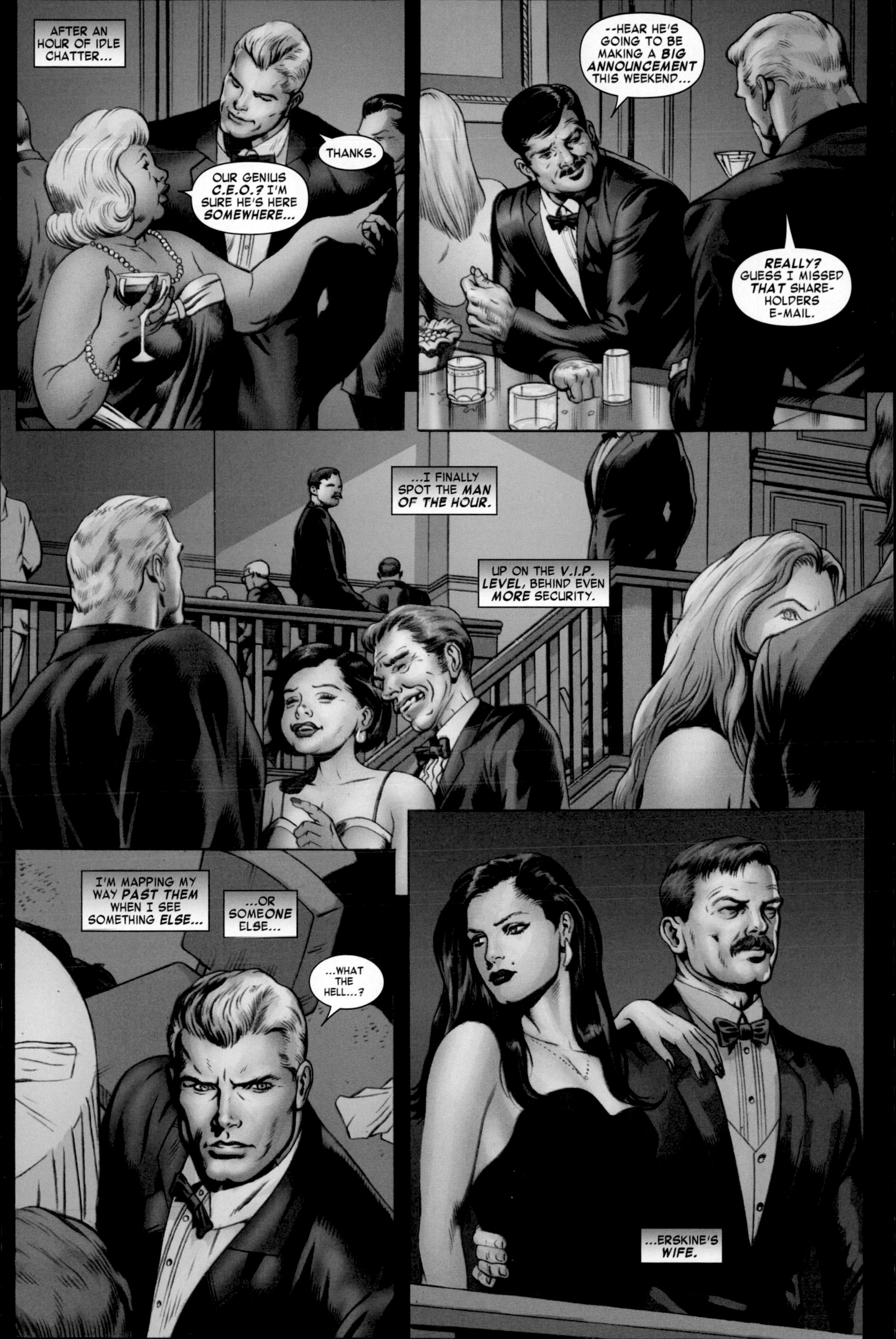
AFTER AN HOUR OF IDLE CHATTER...
THANKS.
OUR GENIUS C.E.O.? I'M SURE HE'S HERE SOMEWHERE...
--HEAR HE'S GOING TO BE MAKING A BIG ANNOUNCEMENT THIS WEEKEND...
REALLY? GUESS I MISSED THAT SHARE-HOLDERS E-MAIL.
...I FINALLY SPOT THE MAN OF THE HOUR.
UP ON THE V.I.P. LEVEL, BEHIND EVEN MORE SECURITY.
I'M MAPPING MY WAY PAST THEM WHEN I SEE SOMETHING ELSE...
...OR SOMEONE ELSE...
...WHAT THE HELL...?
...ERSKINE'S WIFE.

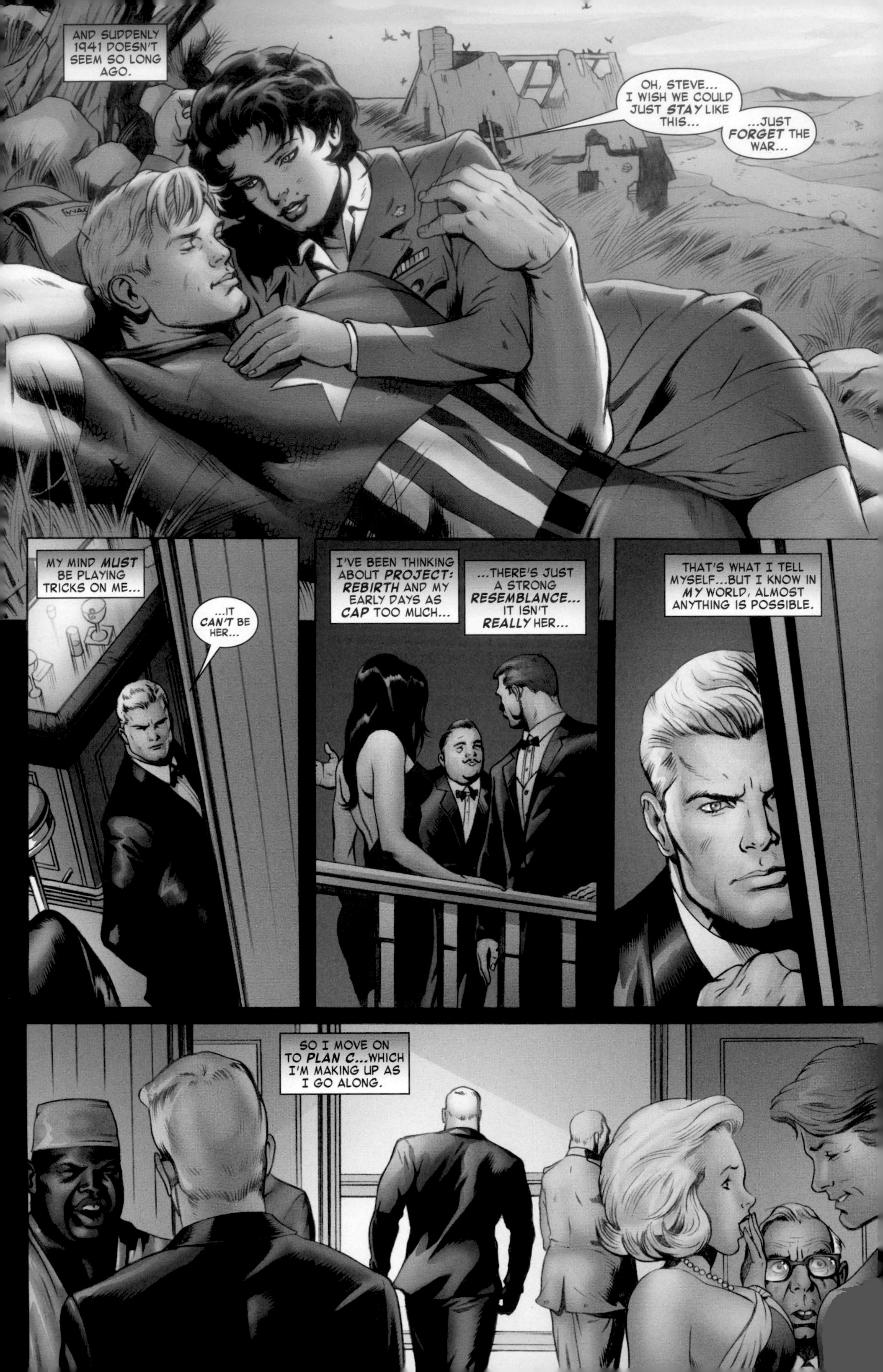
AND SUDDENLY 1941 DOESN'T SEEM SO LONG AGO.
OH, STEVE... I WISH WE COULD JUST STAY LIKE THIS...
...JUST FORGET THE WAR...
MY MIND MUST BE PLAYING TRICKS ON ME...
...IT CAN'T BE HER...
I'VE BEEN THINKING ABOUT PROJECT: REBIRTH AND MY EARLY DAYS AS CAP TOO MUCH...
...THERE'S JUST A STRONG RESEMBLANCE... IT ISN'T REALLY HER...
THAT'S WHAT I TELL MYSELF...BUT I KNOW IN MY WORLD, ALMOST ANYTHING IS POSSIBLE.
SO I MOVE ON TO PLAN C...WHICH I'M MAKING UP AS I GO ALONG.

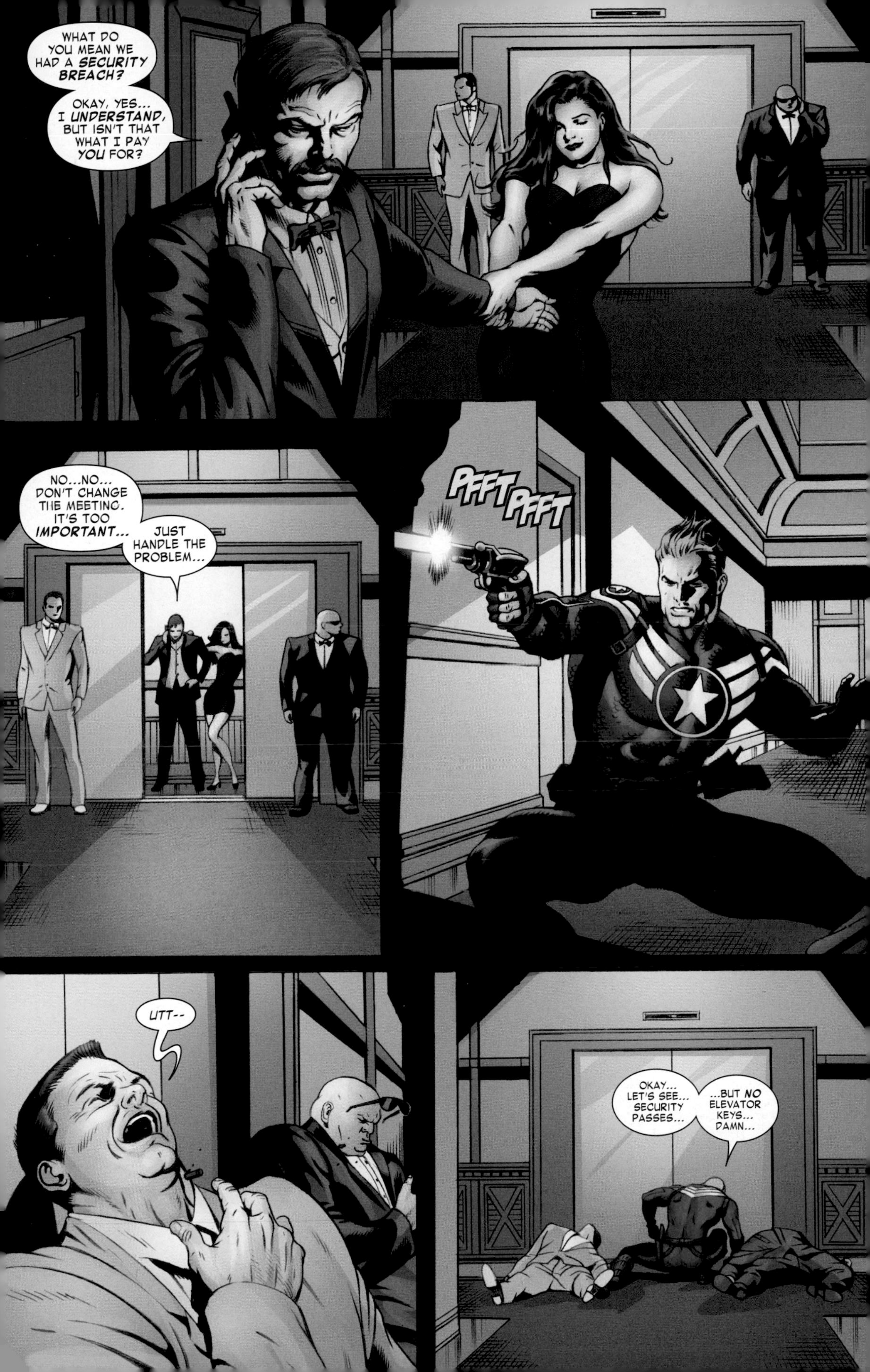
WHAT DO YOU MEAN WE HAD A SECURITY BREACH?
OKAY, YES... I UNDERSTAND, BUT ISN'T THAT WHAT I PAY YOU FOR?
NO...NO... DON'T CHANGE THE MEETING. IT'S TOO IMPORTANT...
JUST HANDLE THE PROBLEM...
PFFT PFFT
UTT--
OKAY... LET'S SEE... SECURITY PASSES...
...BUT NO ELEVATOR KEYS... DAMN...

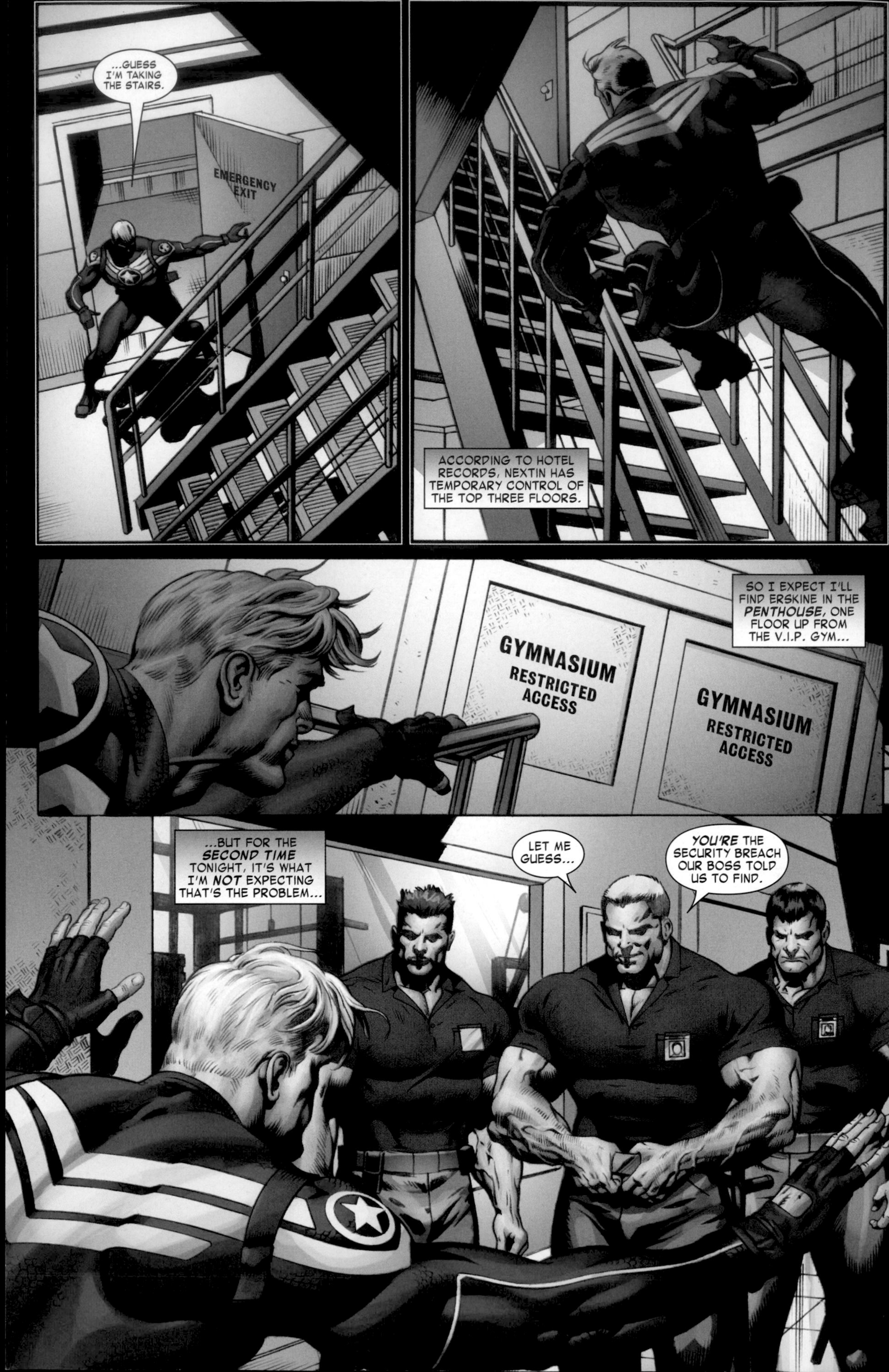
...GUESS I'M TAKING THE STAIRS.
EMERGENCY EXIT
ACCORDING TO HOTEL RECORDS, NEXTIN HAS TEMPORARY CONTROL OF THE TOP THREE FLOORS.
SO I EXPECT I'LL FIND ERSKINE IN THE PENTHOUSE, ONE FLOOR UP FROM THE V.I.P. GYM...
GYMNASIUM RESTRICTED ACCESS
GYMNASIUM RESTRICTED ACCESS
...BUT FOR THE SECOND TIME TONIGHT, IT'S WHAT I'M NOT EXPECTING THAT'S THE PROBLEM...
LET ME GUESS...
YOU'RE THE SECURITY BREACH OUR BOSS TOLD US TO FIND.

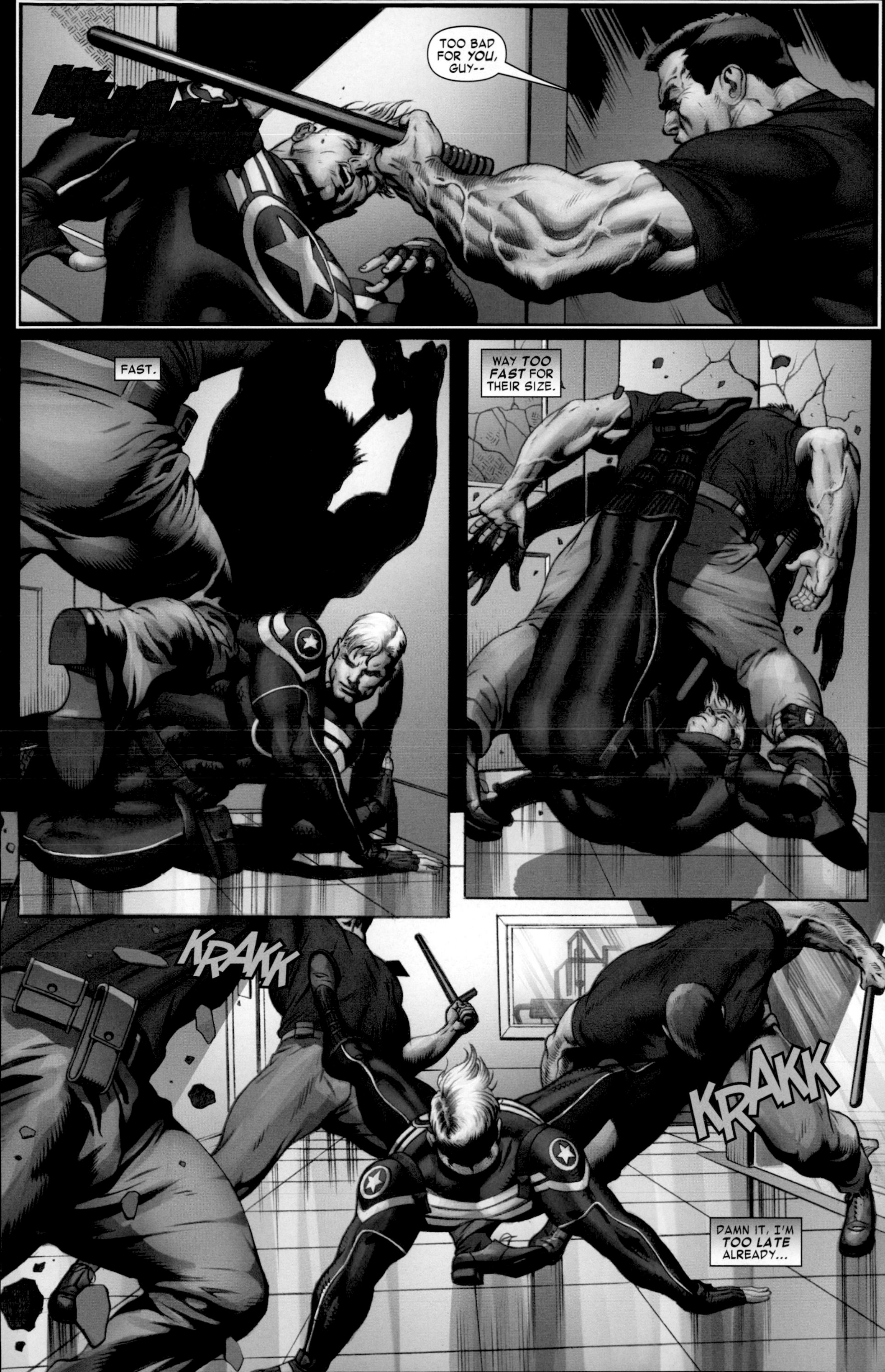

TOO BAD FOR YOU, GUY--
FAST.
WAY TOO FAST FOR THEIR SIZE.
KRAKK
KRAKK
DAMN IT, I'M TOO LATE ALREADY...

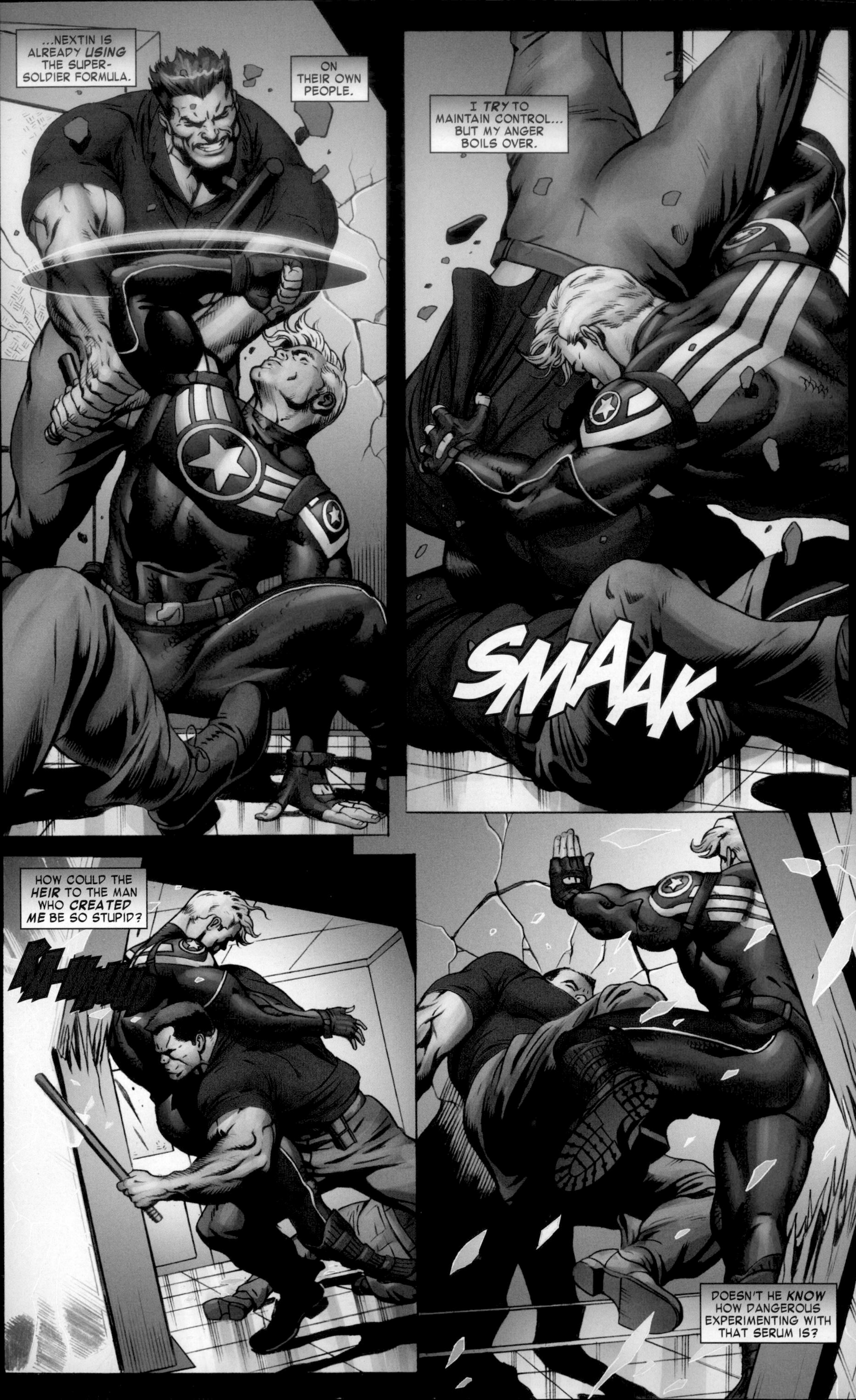
...NEXTIN IS ALREADY USING THE SUPER-SOLDIER FORMULA.
ON THEIR OWN PEOPLE.
I TRY TO MAINTAIN CONTROL... BUT MY ANGER BOILS OVER.
SMAAK
HOW COULD THE HEIR TO THE MAN WHO CREATED ME BE SO STUPID?
DOESN'T HE KNOW HOW DANGEROUS EXPERIMENTING WITH THAT SERUM IS?

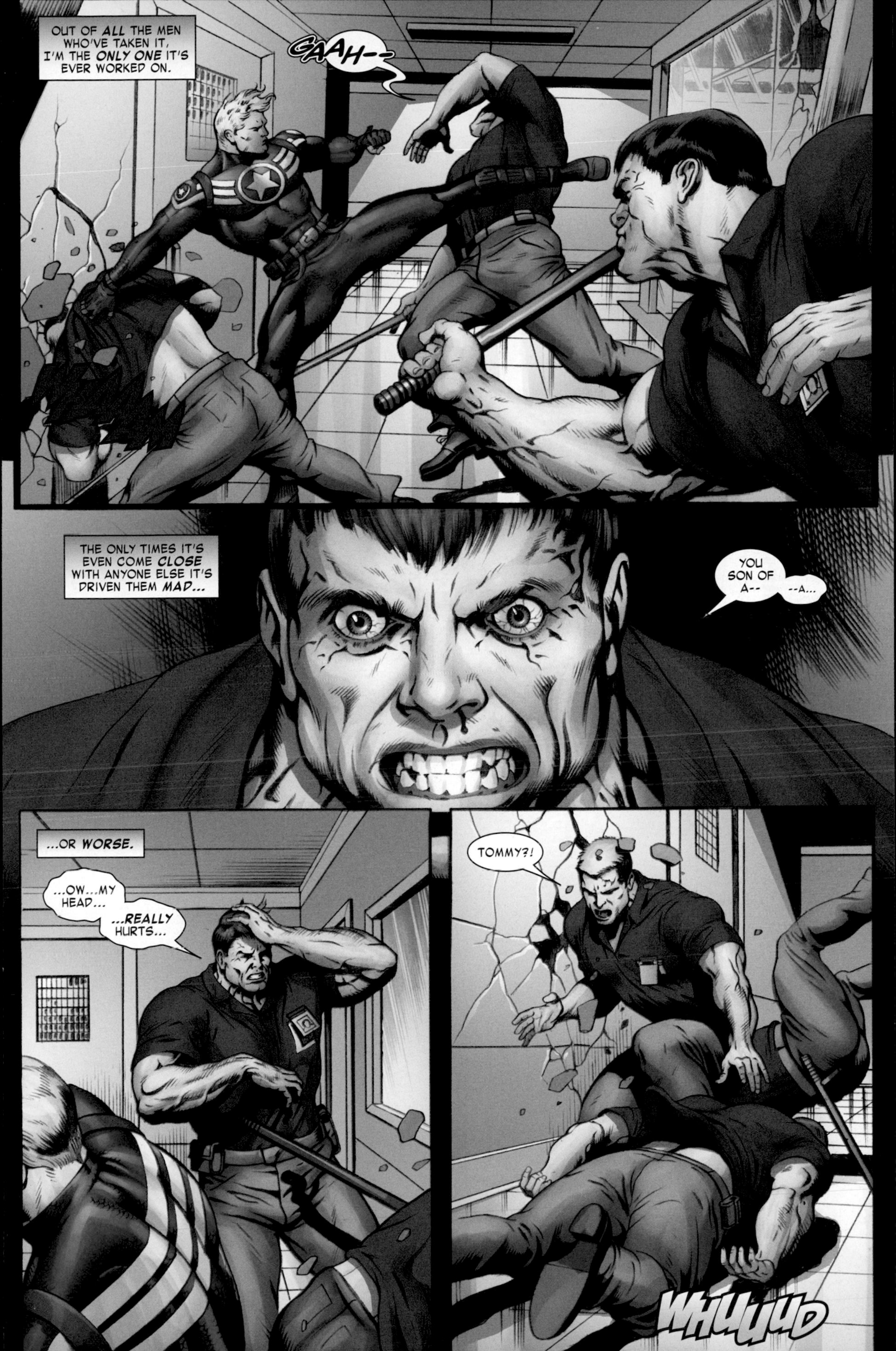
OUT OF ALL THE MEN WHO'VE TAKEN IT, I'M THE ONLY ONE IT'S EVER WORKED ON.
GAAH--
THE ONLY TIMES IT'S EVEN COME CLOSE WITH ANYONE ELSE IT'S DRIVEN THEM MAD...
YOU SON OF A--
--A...
...OR WORSE.
...OW...MY HEAD...
...REALLY HURTS...
TOMMY?!
WHUUUD

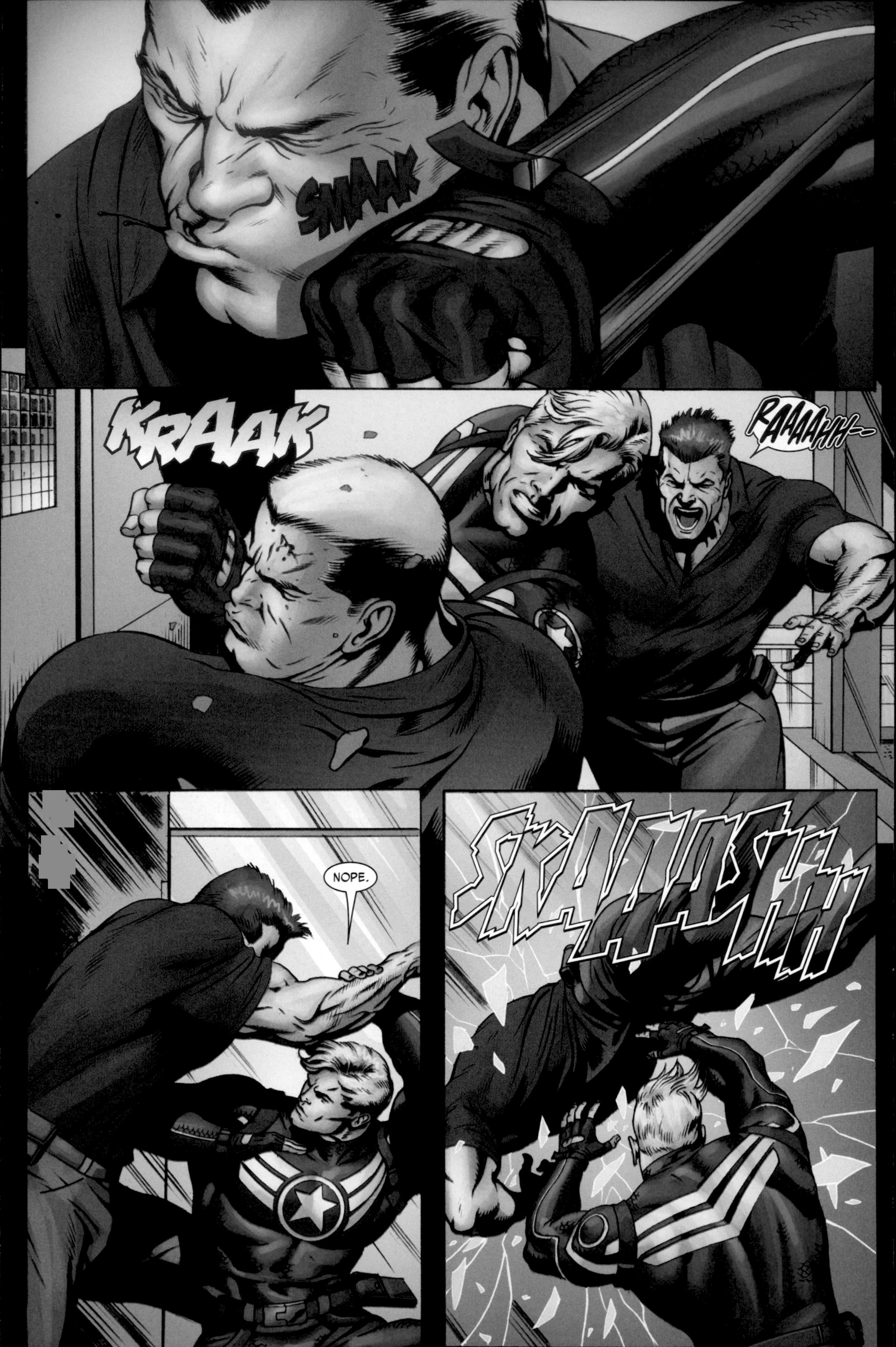
SMAAK
KRAAK
RAAAAHH--
NOPE.
SKRAASH

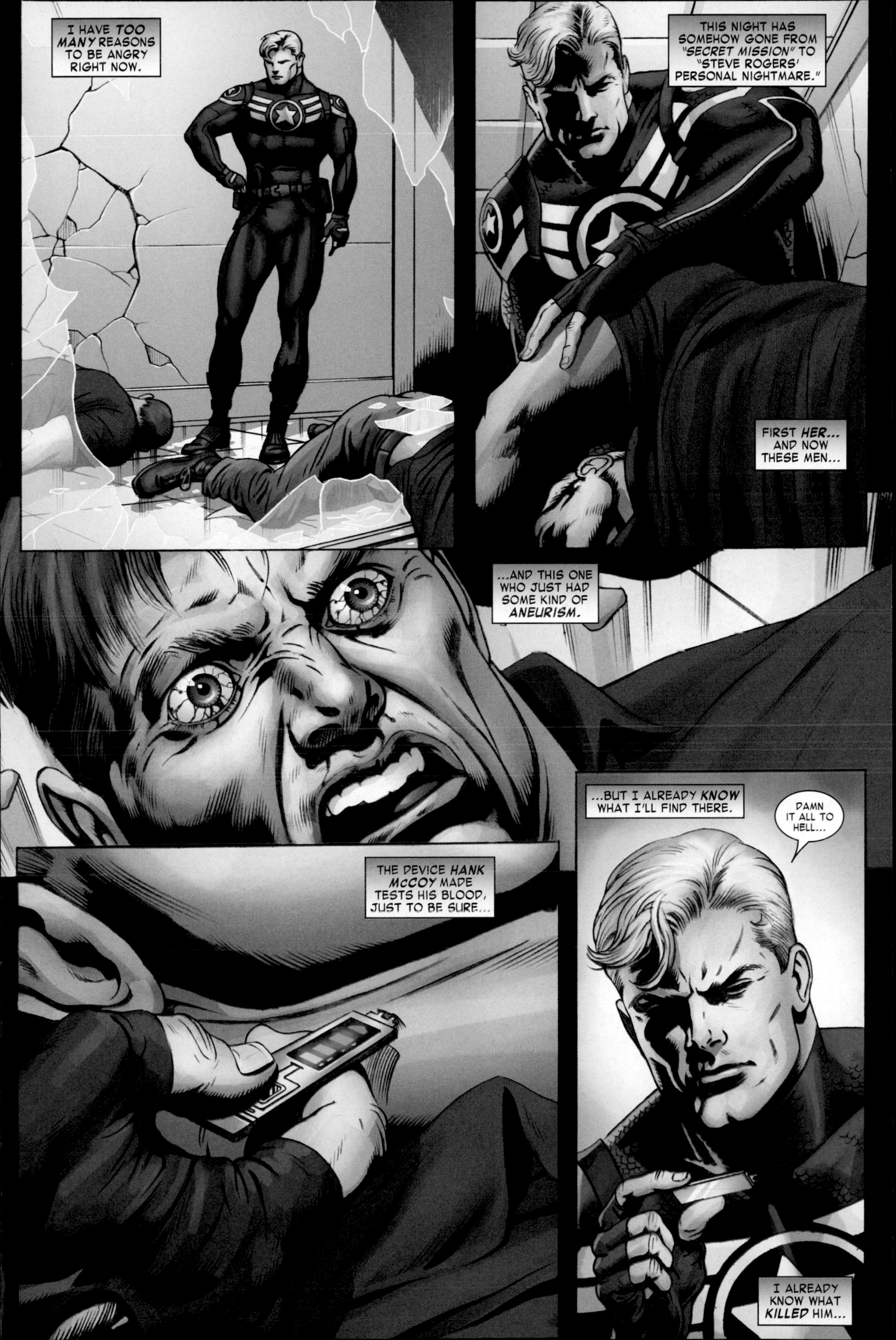
I HAVE TOO MANY REASONS TO BE ANGRY RIGHT NOW.
THIS NIGHT HAS SOMEHOW GONE FROM "SECRET MISSION" TO "STEVE ROGERS' PERSONAL NIGHTMARE."
FIRST HER... AND NOW THESE MEN...
...AND THIS ONE WHO JUST HAD SOME KIND OF ANEURISM.
THE DEVICE HANK McCOY MADE TESTS HIS BLOOD, JUST TO BE SURE...
...BUT I ALREADY KNOW WHAT I'LL FIND THERE.
DAMN IT ALL TO HELL...
I ALREADY KNOW WHAT KILLED HIM...

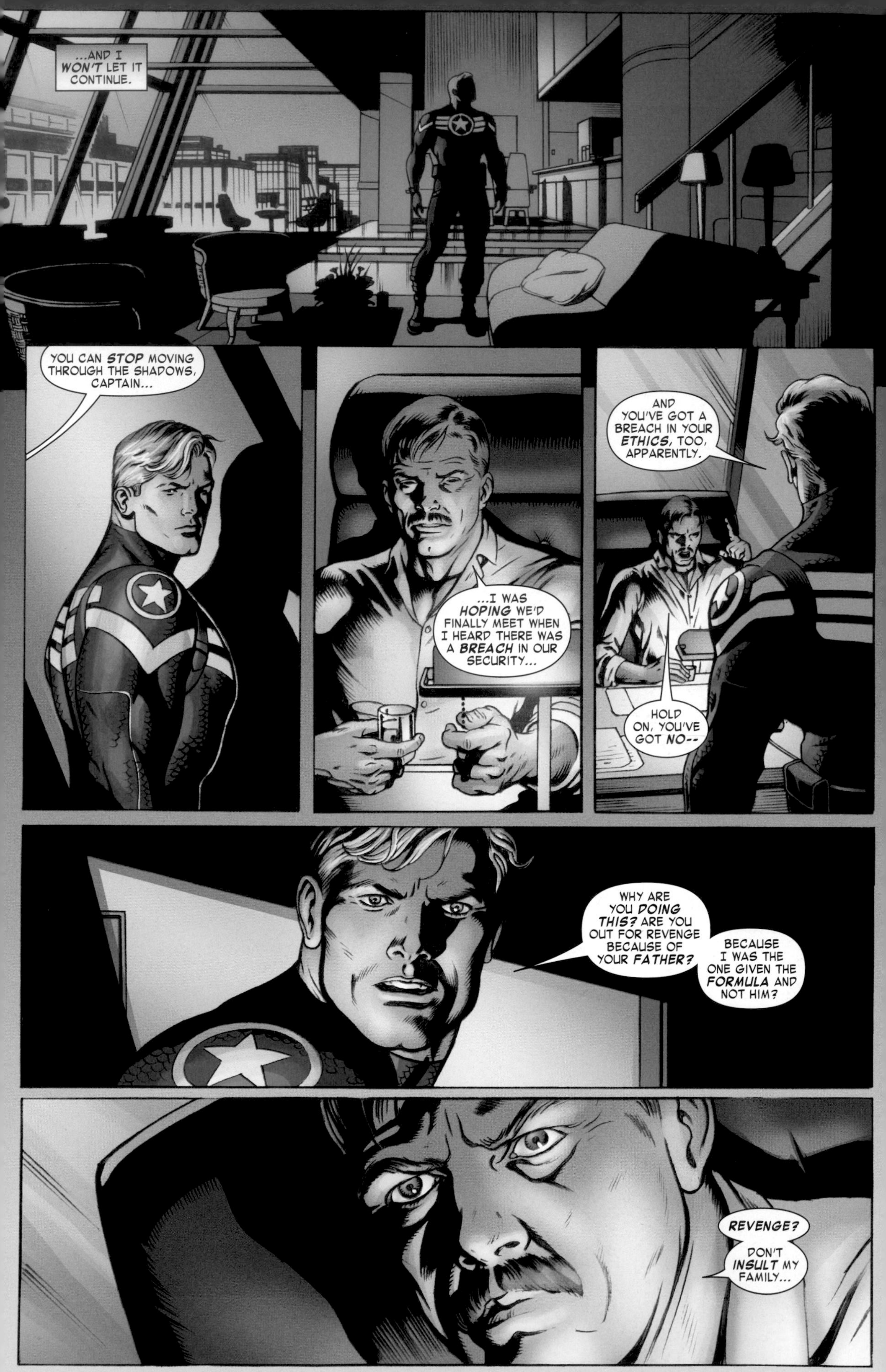

...AND I WON'T LET IT CONTINUE.
YOU CAN STOP MOVING THROUGH THE SHADOWS, CAPTAIN...
...I WAS HOPING WE'D FINALLY MEET WHEN I HEARD THERE WAS A BREACH IN OUR SECURITY...
AND YOU'VE GOT A BREACH IN YOUR ETHICS, TOO, APPARENTLY.
HOLD ON, YOU'VE GOT NO--
WHY ARE YOU DOING THIS? ARE YOU OUT FOR REVENGE BECAUSE OF YOUR FATHER?
BECAUSE I WAS THE ONE GIVEN THE FORMULA AND NOT HIM?
REVENGE?
DON'T INSULT MY FAMILY...

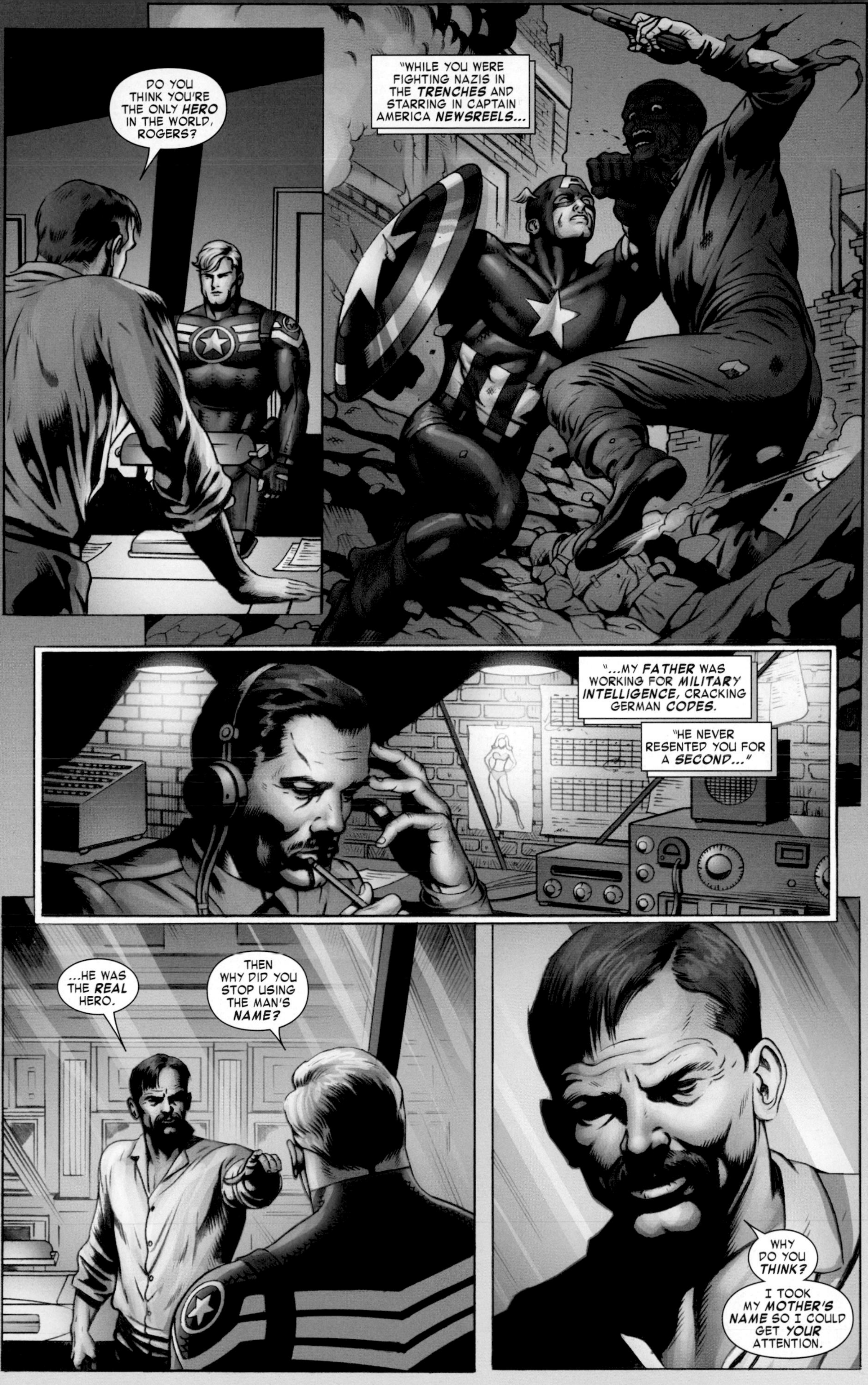
DO YOU THINK YOU'RE THE ONLY HERO IN THE WORLD, ROGERS?
"WHILE YOU WERE FIGHTING NAZIS IN THE TRENCHES AND STARRING IN CAPTAIN AMERICA NEWSREELS...
"...MY FATHER WAS WORKING FOR MILITARY INTELLIGENCE, CRACKING GERMAN CODES.
"HE NEVER RESENTED YOU FOR A SECOND..."
...HE WAS THE REAL HERO.
THEN WHY DID YOU STOP USING THE MAN'S NAME?
WHY DO YOU THINK?
I TOOK MY MOTHER'S NAME SO I COULD GET YOUR ATTENTION.

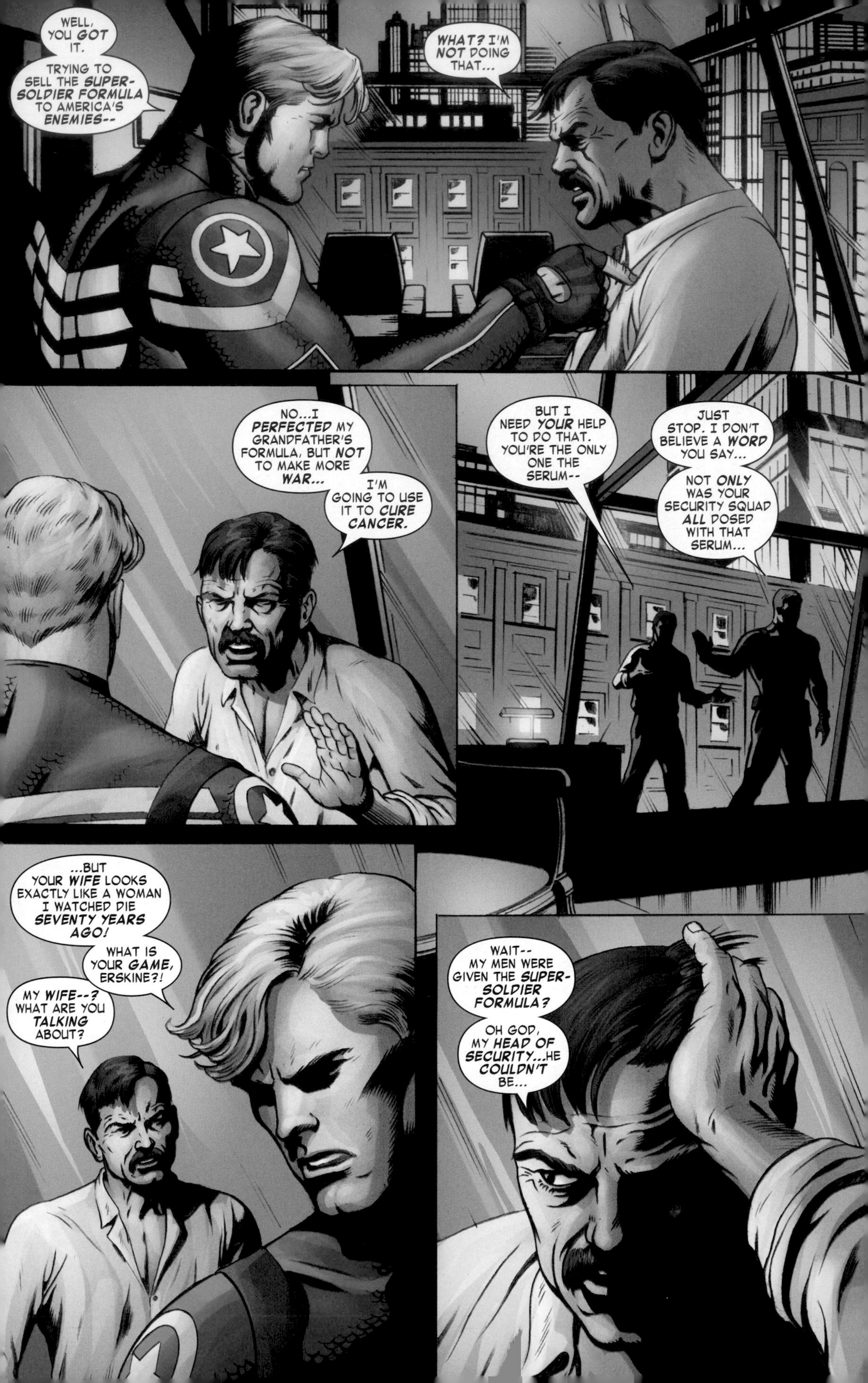
WELL, YOU GOT IT.
TRYING TO SELL THE SUPER-SOLDIER FORMULA TO AMERICA'S ENEMIES--
WHAT? I'M NOT DOING THAT...
NO...I PERFECTED MY GRANDFATHER'S FORMULA, BUT NOT TO MAKE MORE WAR...
I'M GOING TO USE IT TO CURE CANCER.
BUT I NEED YOUR HELP TO DO THAT. YOU'RE THE ONLY ONE THE SERUM--
JUST STOP. I DON'T BELIEVE A WORD YOU SAY...
NOT ONLY WAS YOUR SECURITY SQUAD ALL DOSED WITH THAT SERUM...
...BUT YOUR WIFE LOOKS EXACTLY LIKE A WOMAN I WATCHED DIE SEVENTY YEARS AGO!
WHAT IS YOUR GAME, ERSKINE?!
MY WIFE--? WHAT ARE YOU TALKING ABOUT?
WAIT-- MY MEN WERE GIVEN THE SUPER-SOLDIER FORMULA?
OH GOD, MY HEAD OF SECURITY...HE COULDN'T BE...

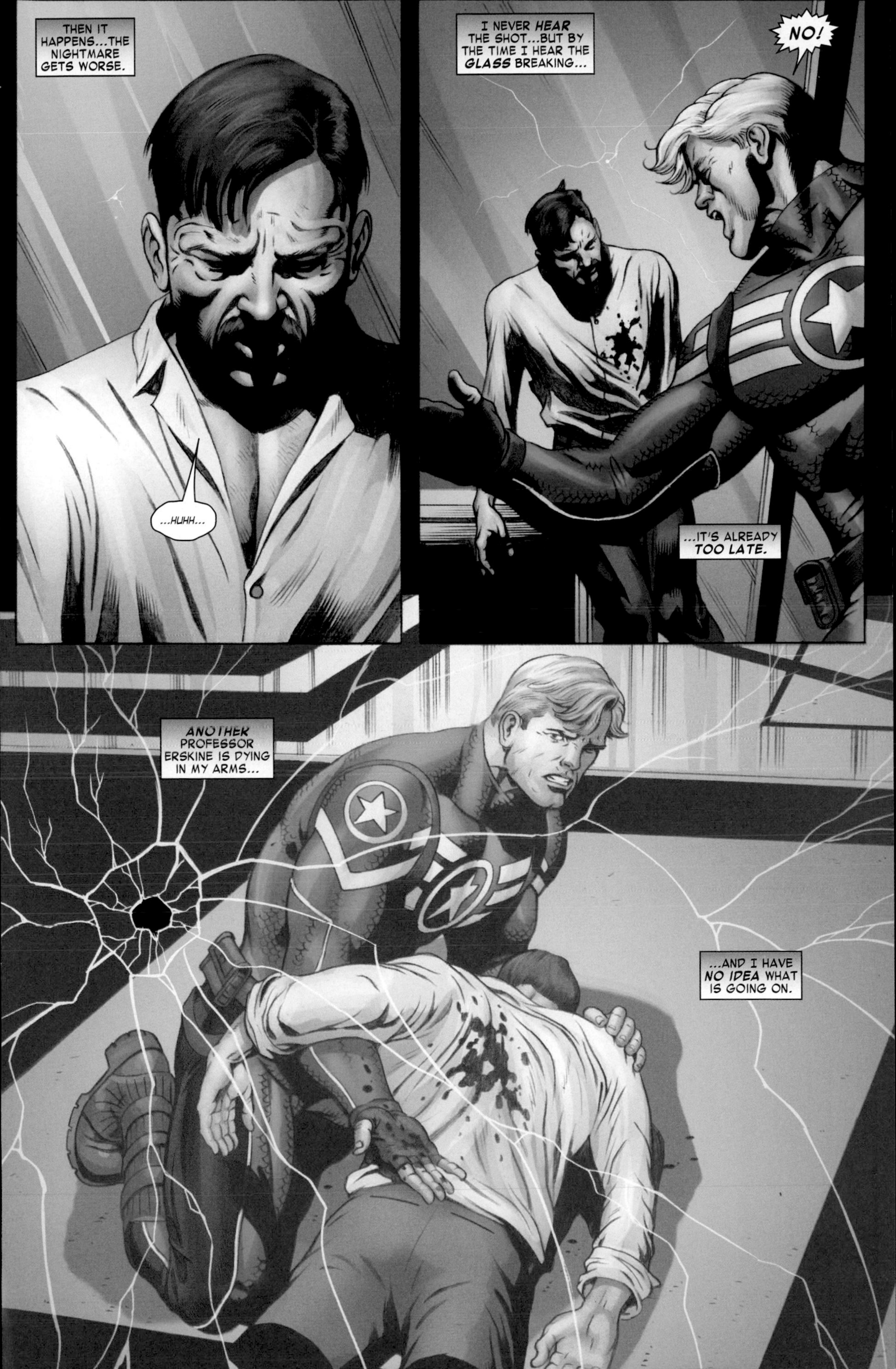
THEN IT HAPPENS...THE NIGHTMARE GETS WORSE.
...HUHH...
I NEVER HEAR THE SHOT...BUT BY THE TIME I HEAR THE GLASS BREAKING...
NO!
...IT'S ALREADY TOO LATE.
ANOTHER PROFESSOR ERSKINE IS DYING IN MY ARMS...
...AND I HAVE NO IDEA WHAT IS GOING ON.

2

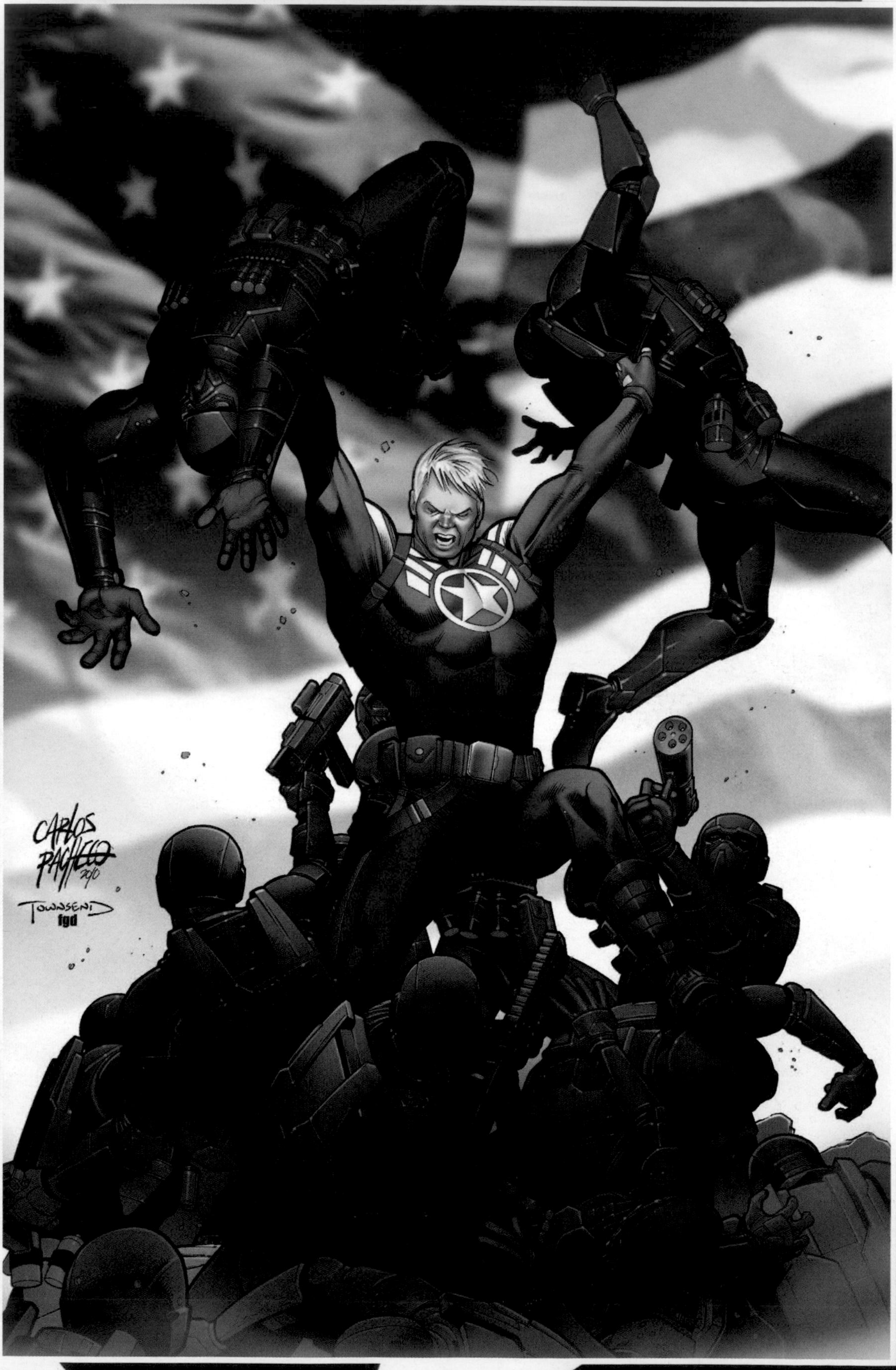
CARLOS PACHECO 2010
TOWNSEND
fgd

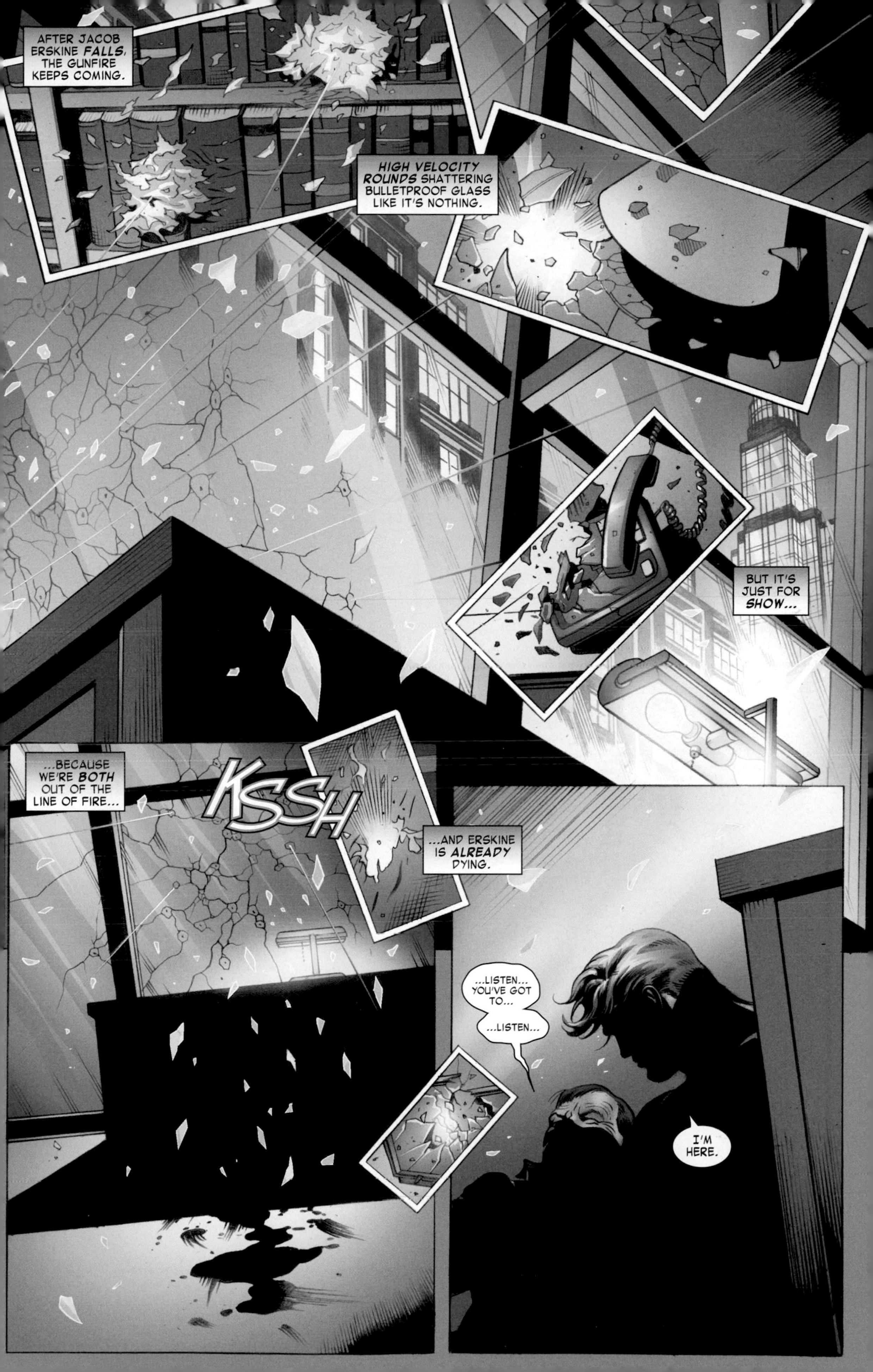
AFTER JACOB ERSKINE *FALLS*, THE GUNFIRE KEEPS COMING.
HIGH VELOCITY ROUNDS SHATTERING BULLETPROOF GLASS LIKE IT'S NOTHING.
BUT IT'S JUST FOR *SHOW*...
...BECAUSE WE'RE *BOTH* OUT OF THE LINE OF FIRE...
KSSH
...AND ERSKINE IS *ALREADY* DYING.
...LISTEN... YOU'VE GOT TO...
...LISTEN...
I'M HERE.

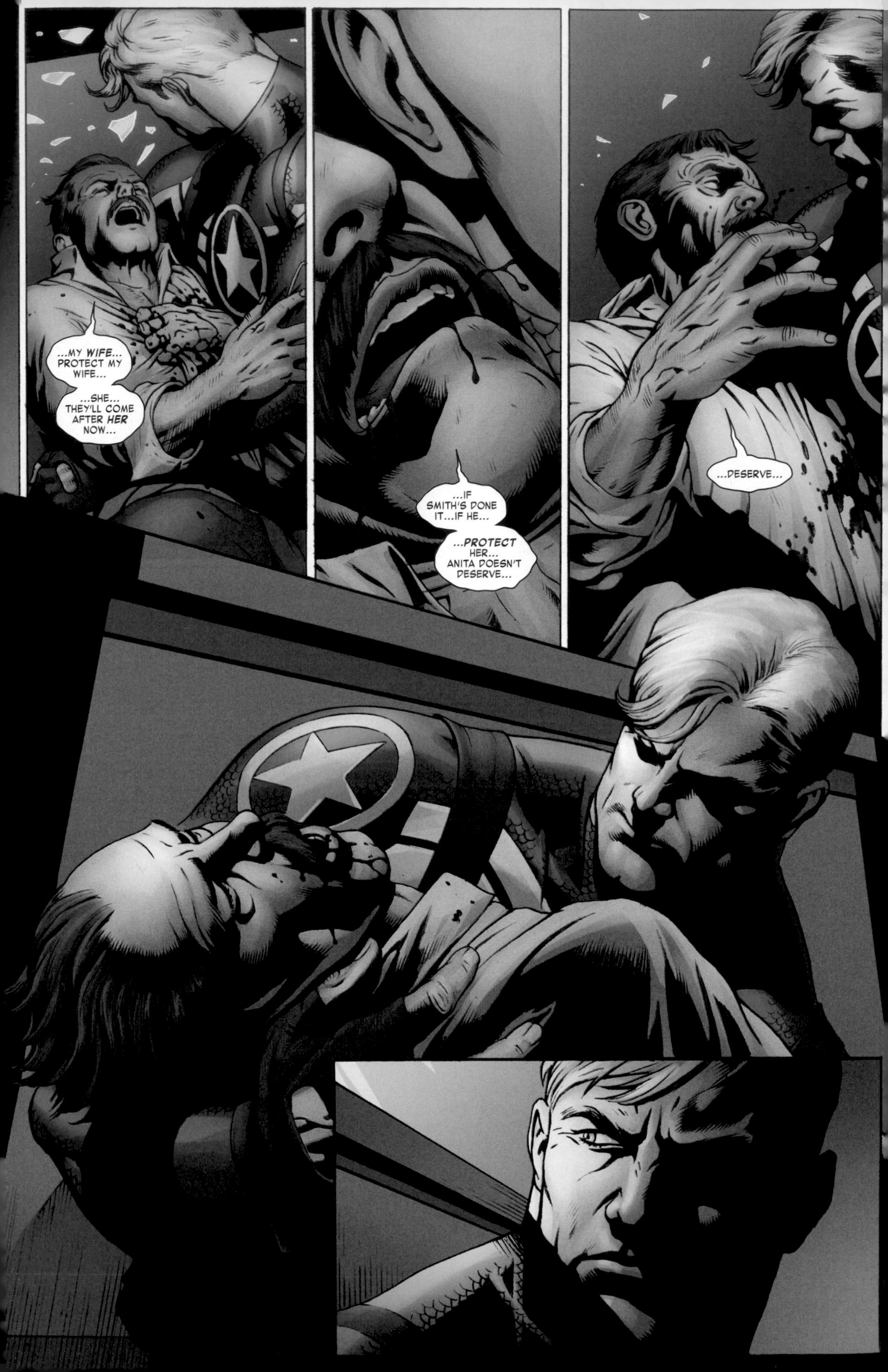
...MY WIFE... PROTECT MY WIFE...
...SHE... THEY'LL COME AFTER HER NOW...
...IF SMITH'S DONE IT...IF HE...
...PROTECT HER... ANITA DOESN'T DESERVE...
...DESERVE...

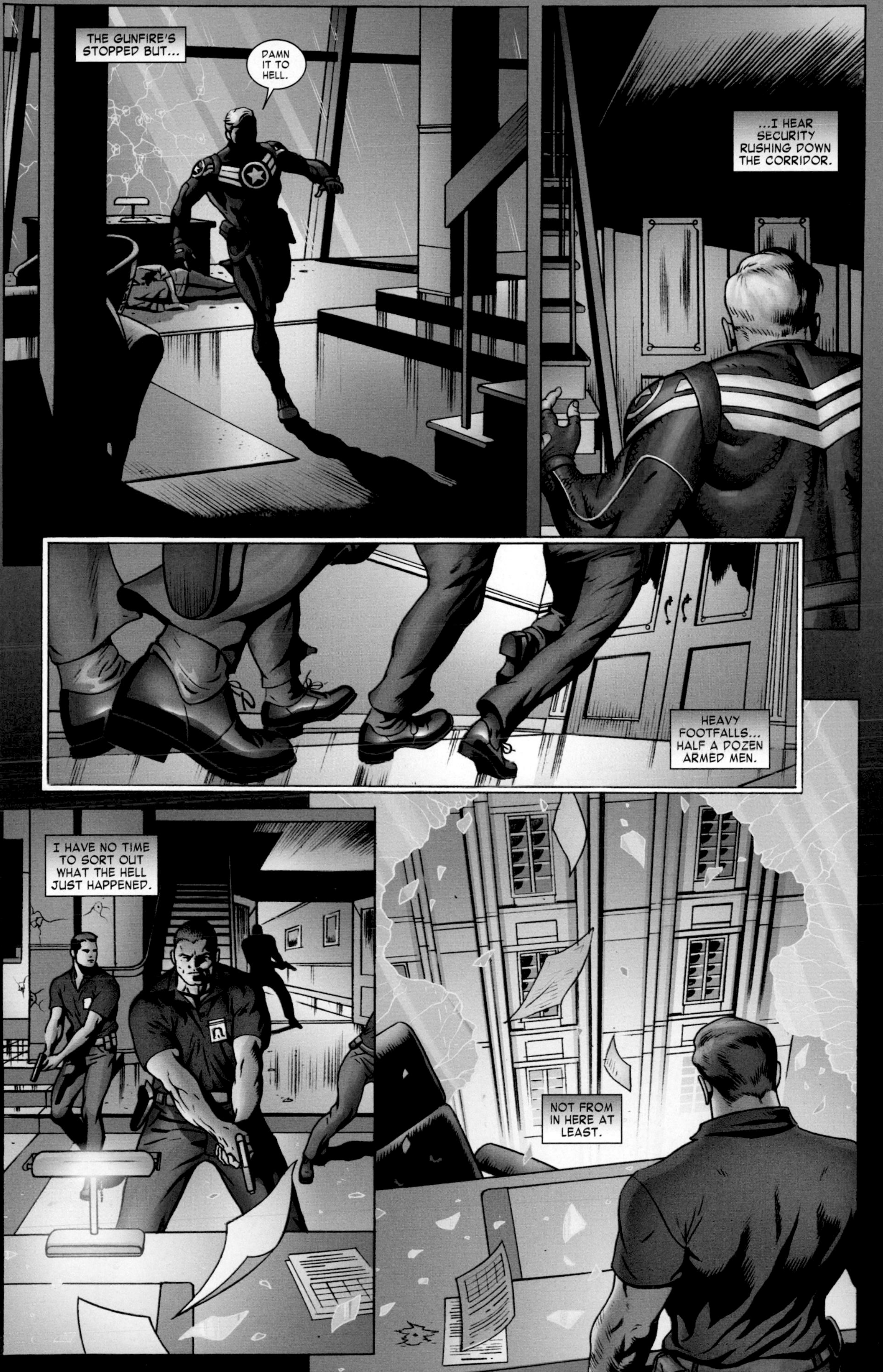
THE GUNFIRE'S STOPPED BUT...
DAMN IT TO HELL.
...I HEAR SECURITY RUSHING DOWN THE CORRIDOR.
HEAVY FOOTFALLS... HALF A DOZEN ARMED MEN.
I HAVE NO TIME TO SORT OUT WHAT THE HELL JUST HAPPENED.
NOT FROM IN HERE AT LEAST.

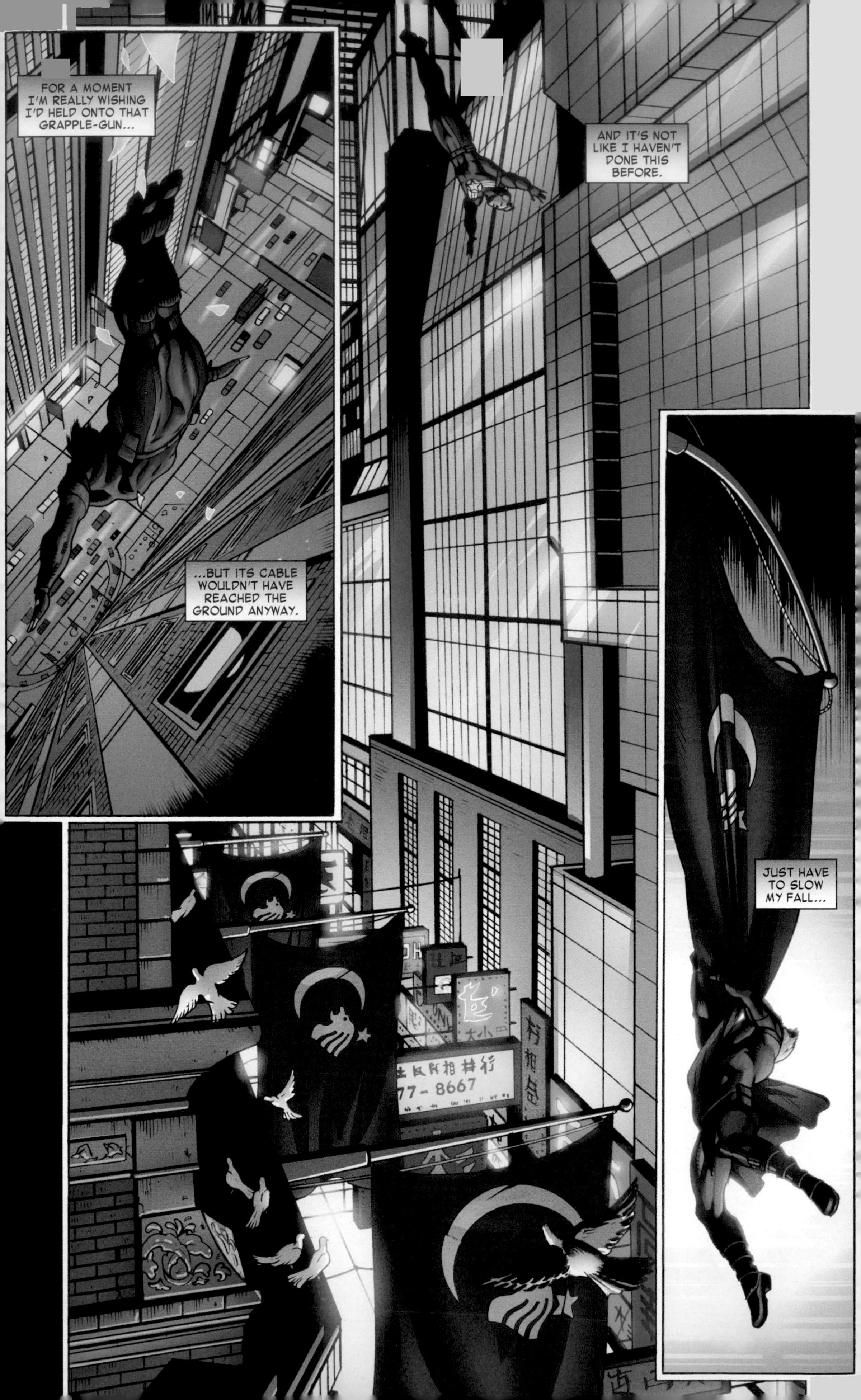
FOR A MOMENT I'M REALLY WISHING I'D HELD ONTO THAT GRAPPLE-GUN...
...BUT ITS CABLE WOULDN'T HAVE REACHED THE GROUND ANYWAY.
AND IT'S NOT LIKE I HAVEN'T DONE THIS BEFORE.
JUST HAVE TO SLOW MY FALL...
77-8667

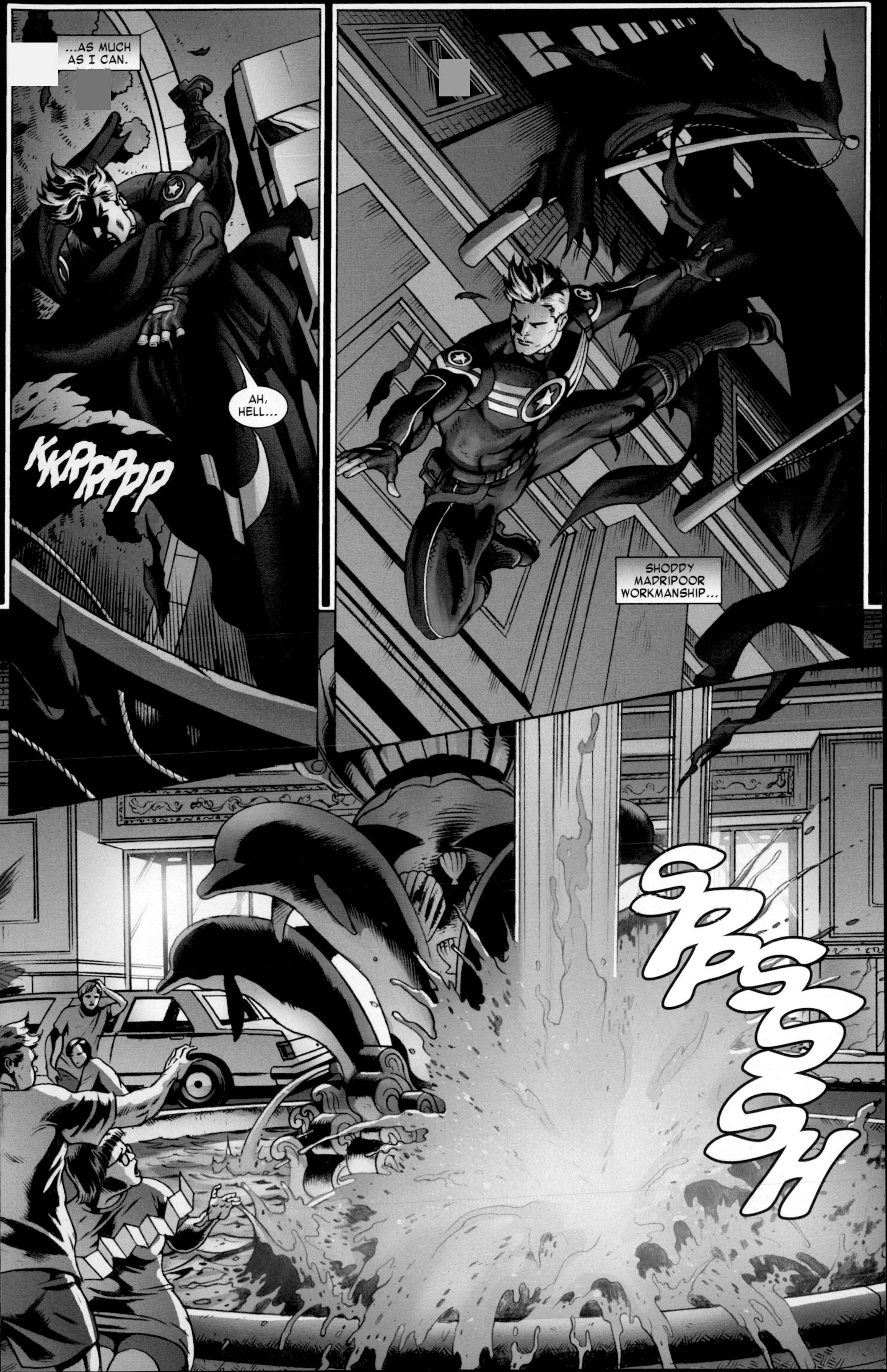
...AS MUCH AS I CAN.
AH, HELL...
KKRRPPP
SHODDY MADRIPOOR WORKMANSHIP...
SPLSSSH

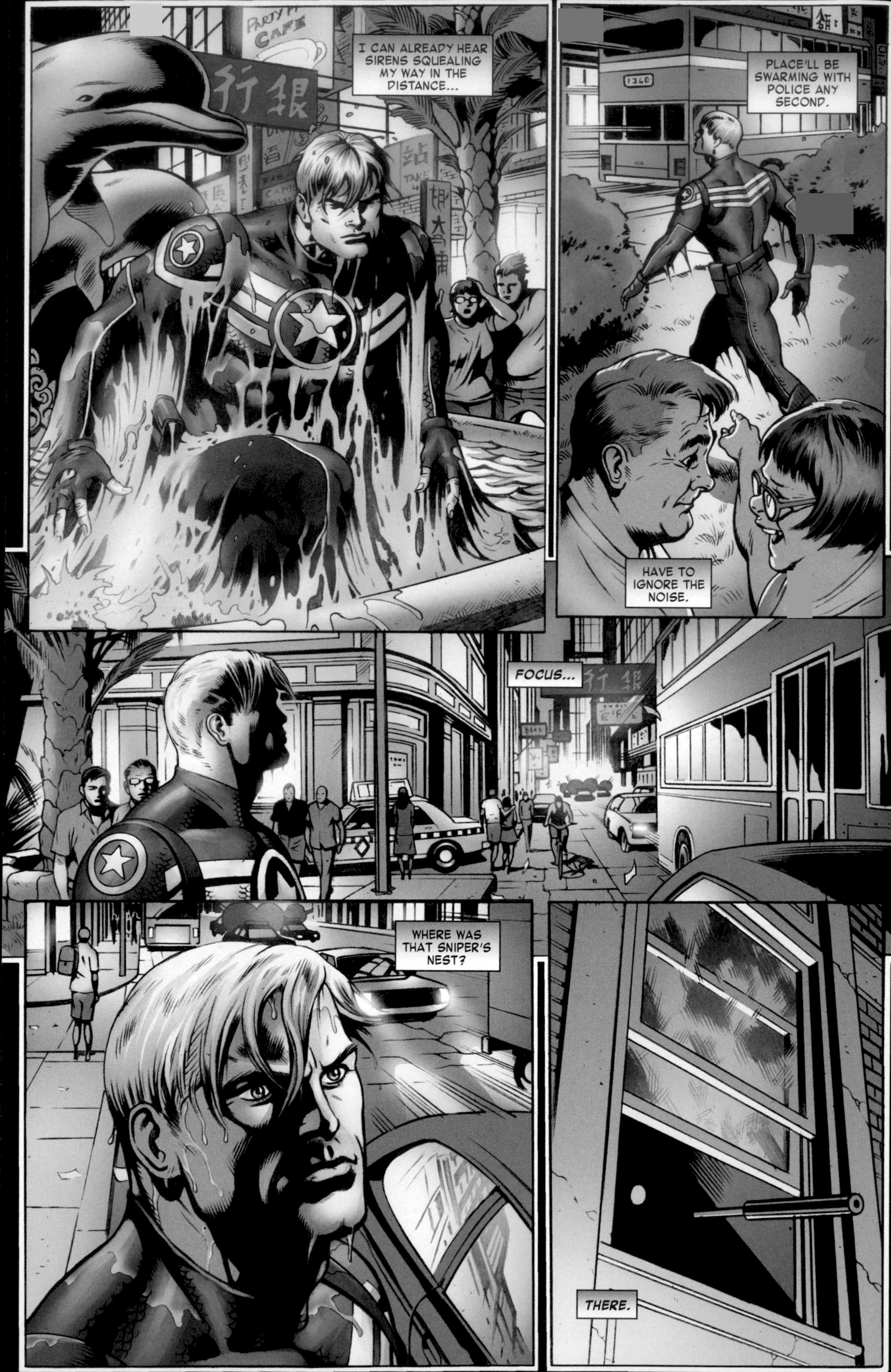
I CAN ALREADY HEAR SIRENS SQUEALING MY WAY IN THE DISTANCE...
PLACE'LL BE SWARMING WITH POLICE ANY SECOND.
HAVE TO IGNORE THE NOISE.
FOCUS...
WHERE WAS THAT SNIPER'S NEST?
THERE.

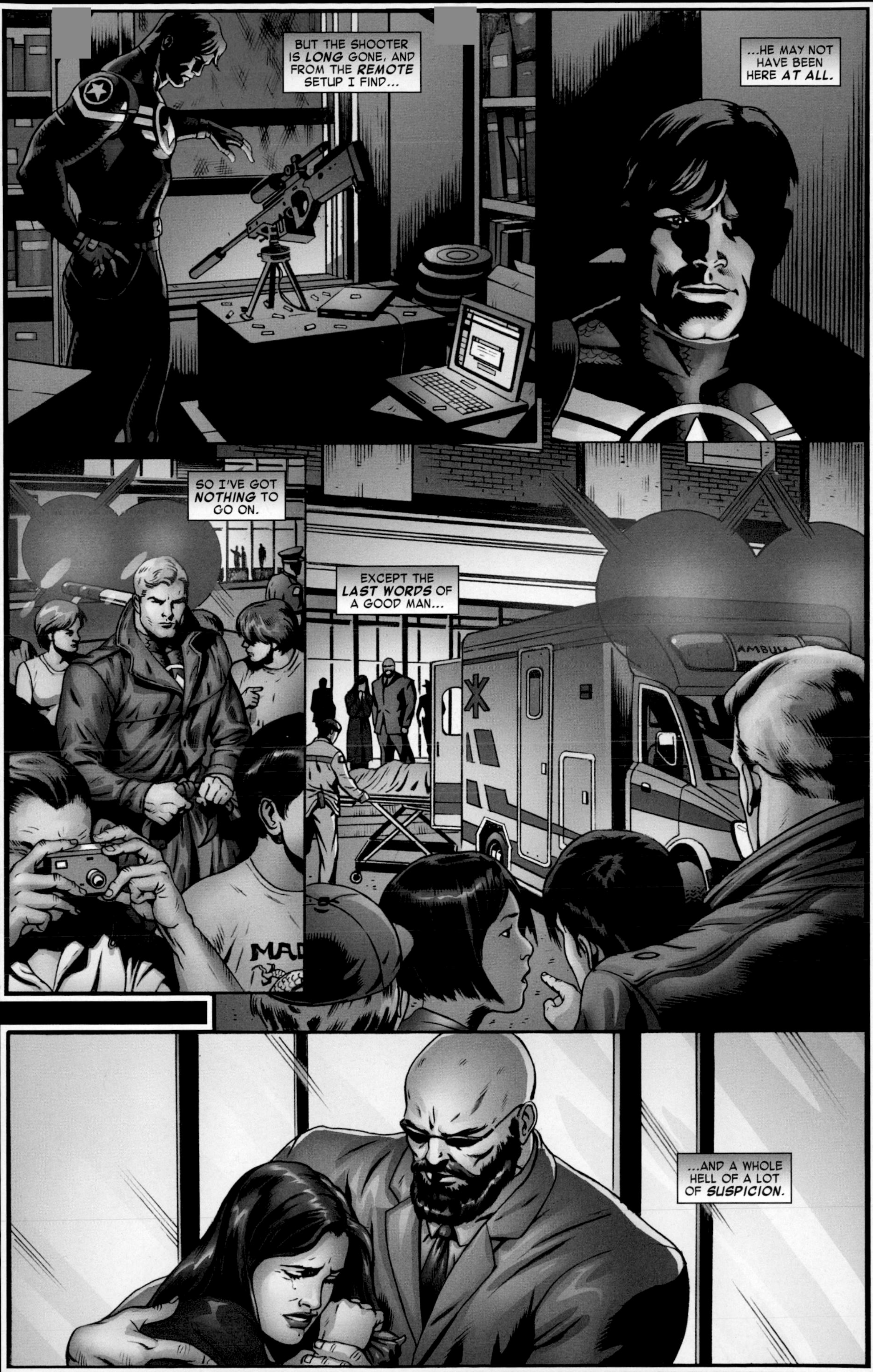
BUT THE SHOOTER IS LONG GONE, AND FROM THE REMOTE SETUP I FIND...
...HE MAY NOT HAVE BEEN HERE AT ALL.
SO I'VE GOT NOTHING TO GO ON.
EXCEPT THE LAST WORDS OF A GOOD MAN...
...AND A WHOLE HELL OF A LOT OF SUSPICION.

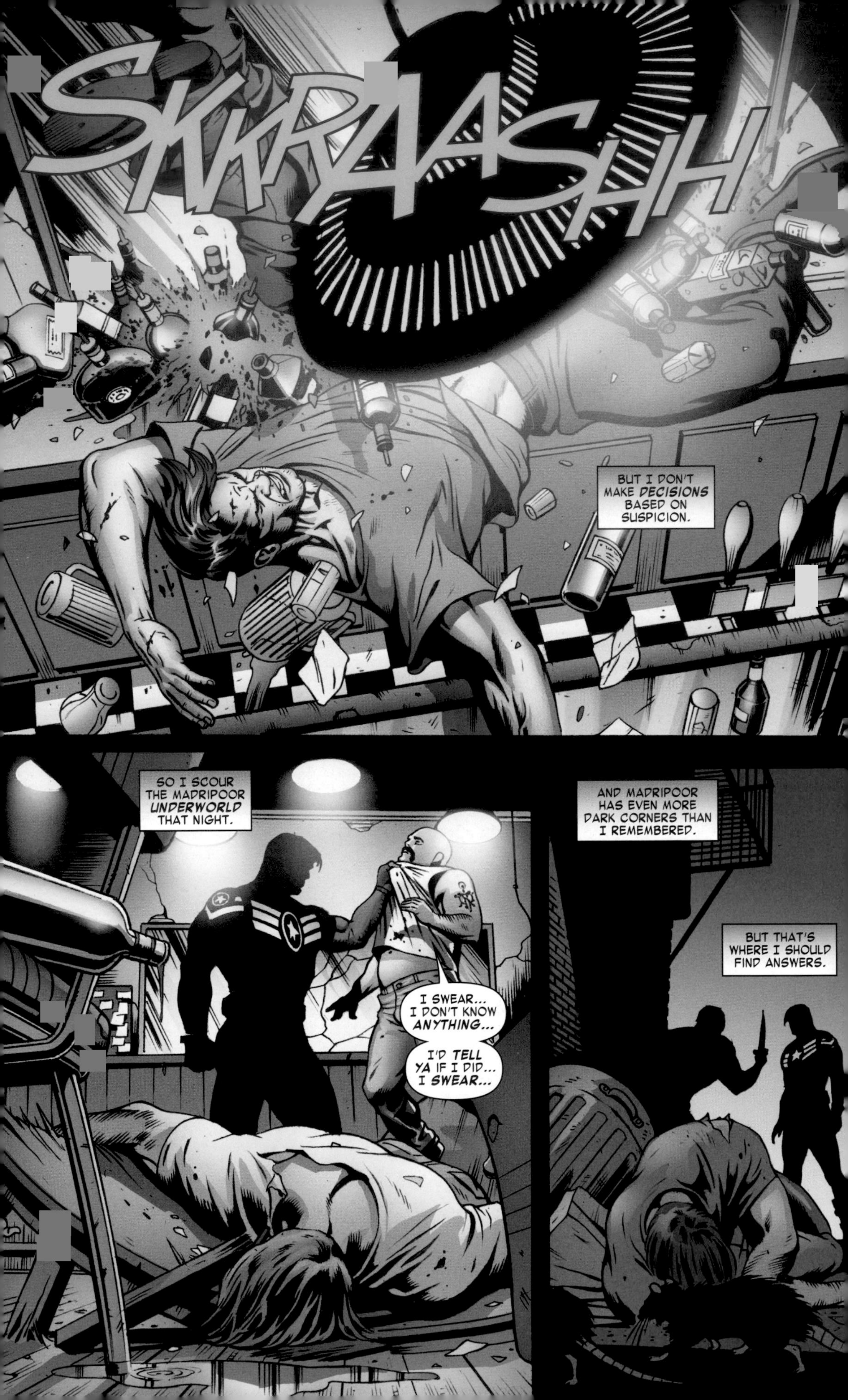
SKKRAASHH
BUT I DON'T MAKE DECISIONS BASED ON SUSPICION.
SO I SCOUR THE MADRIPOOR UNDERWORLD THAT NIGHT.
I SWEAR... I DON'T KNOW ANYTHING...
I'D TELL YA IF I DID... I SWEAR...
AND MADRIPOOR HAS EVEN MORE DARK CORNERS THAN I REMEMBERED.
BUT THAT'S WHERE I SHOULD FIND ANSWERS.

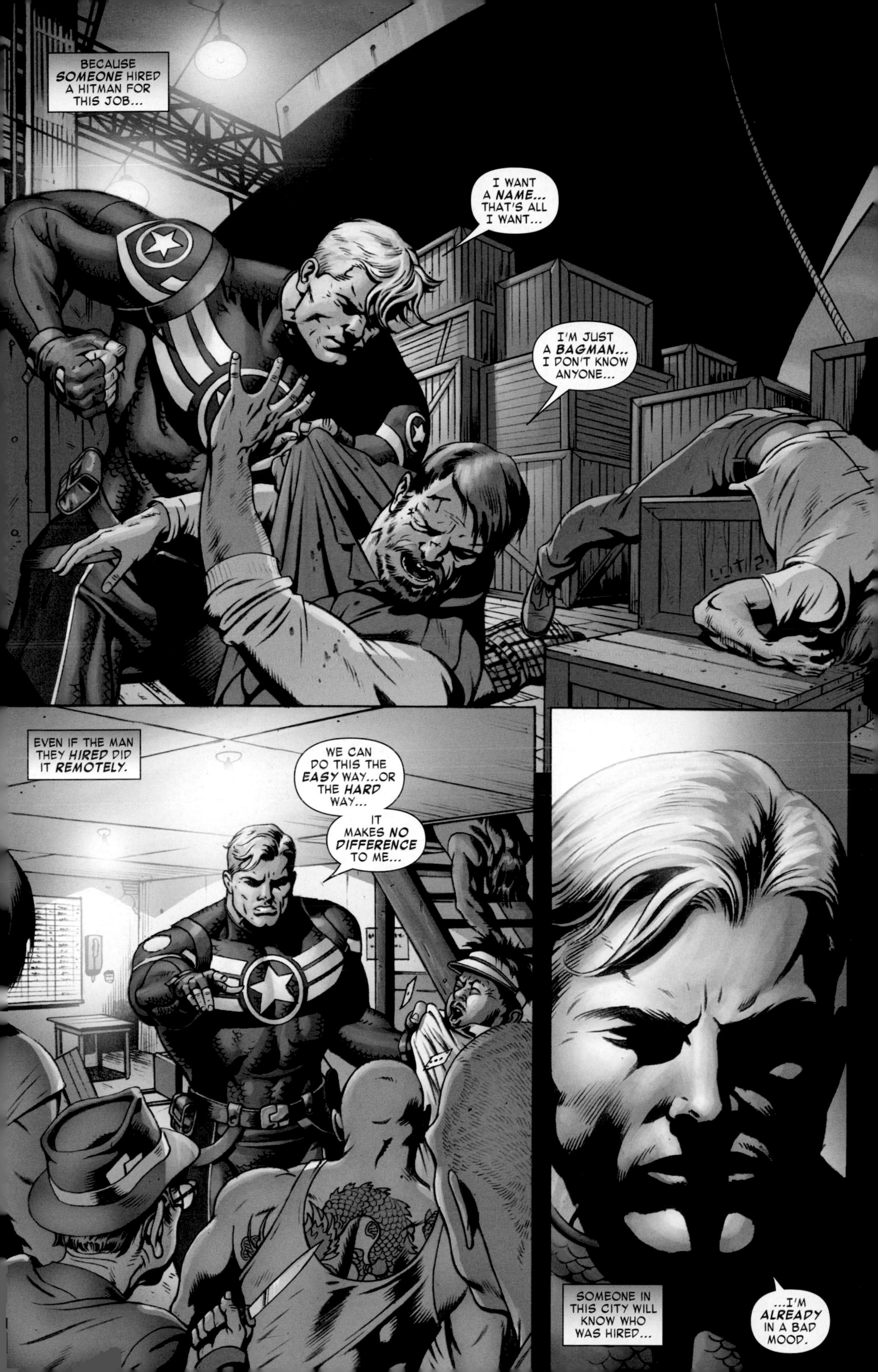
BECAUSE SOMEONE HIRED A HITMAN FOR THIS JOB...
I WANT A NAME... THAT'S ALL I WANT...
I'M JUST A BAGMAN... I DON'T KNOW ANYONE...
EVEN IF THE MAN THEY HIRED DID IT REMOTELY.
WE CAN DO THIS THE EASY WAY...OR THE HARD WAY...
IT MAKES NO DIFFERENCE TO ME...
SOMEONE IN THIS CITY WILL KNOW WHO WAS HIRED...
...I'M ALREADY IN A BAD MOOD.

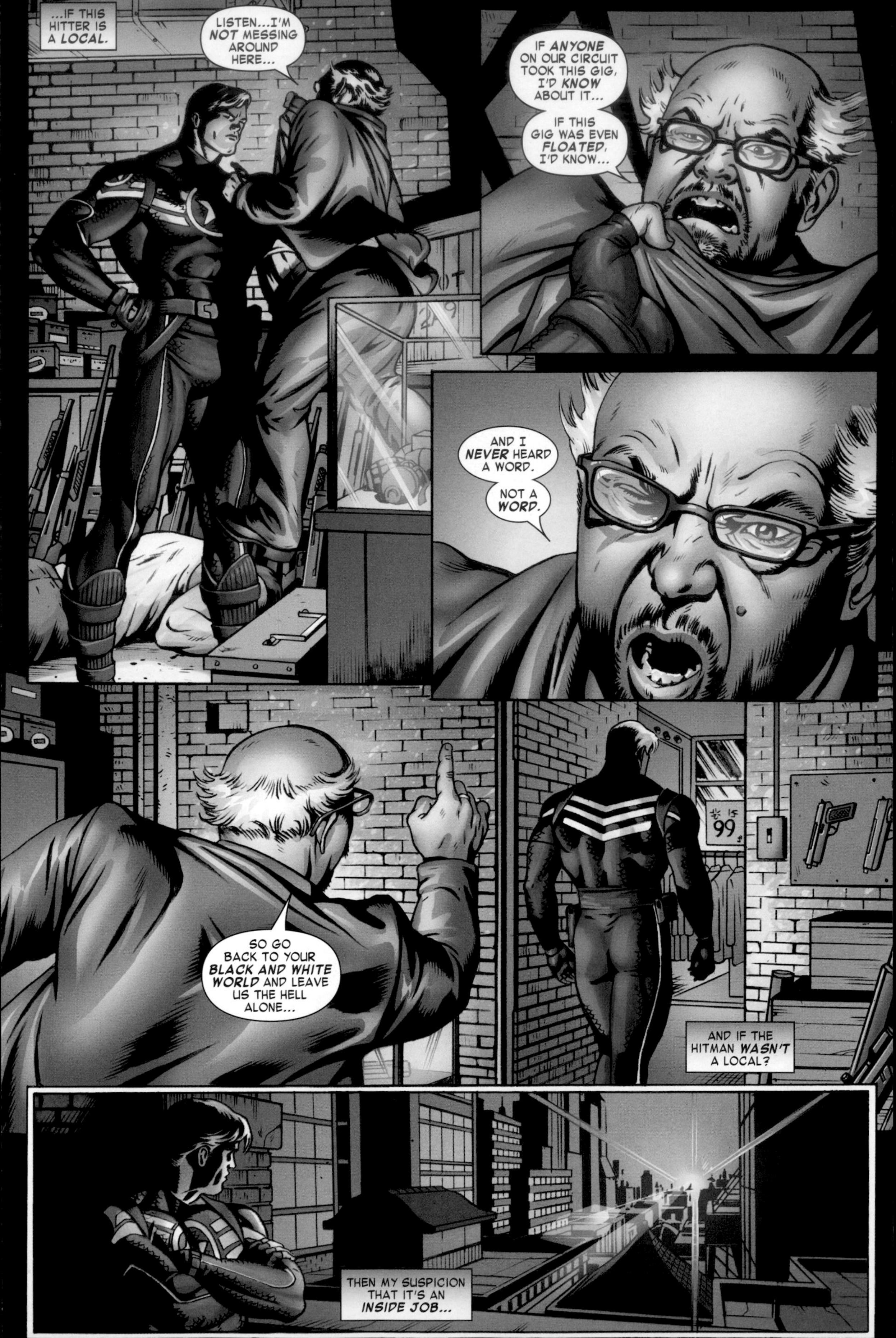
...IF THIS HITTER IS A LOCAL.
LISTEN...I'M NOT MESSING AROUND HERE...
IF ANYONE ON OUR CIRCUIT TOOK THIS GIG, I'D KNOW ABOUT IT...
IF THIS GIG WAS EVEN FLOATED, I'D KNOW...
AND I NEVER HEARD A WORD.
NOT A WORD.
SO GO BACK TO YOUR BLACK AND WHITE WORLD AND LEAVE US THE HELL ALONE...
AND IF THE HITMAN WASN'T A LOCAL?
THEN MY SUSPICION THAT IT'S AN INSIDE JOB...

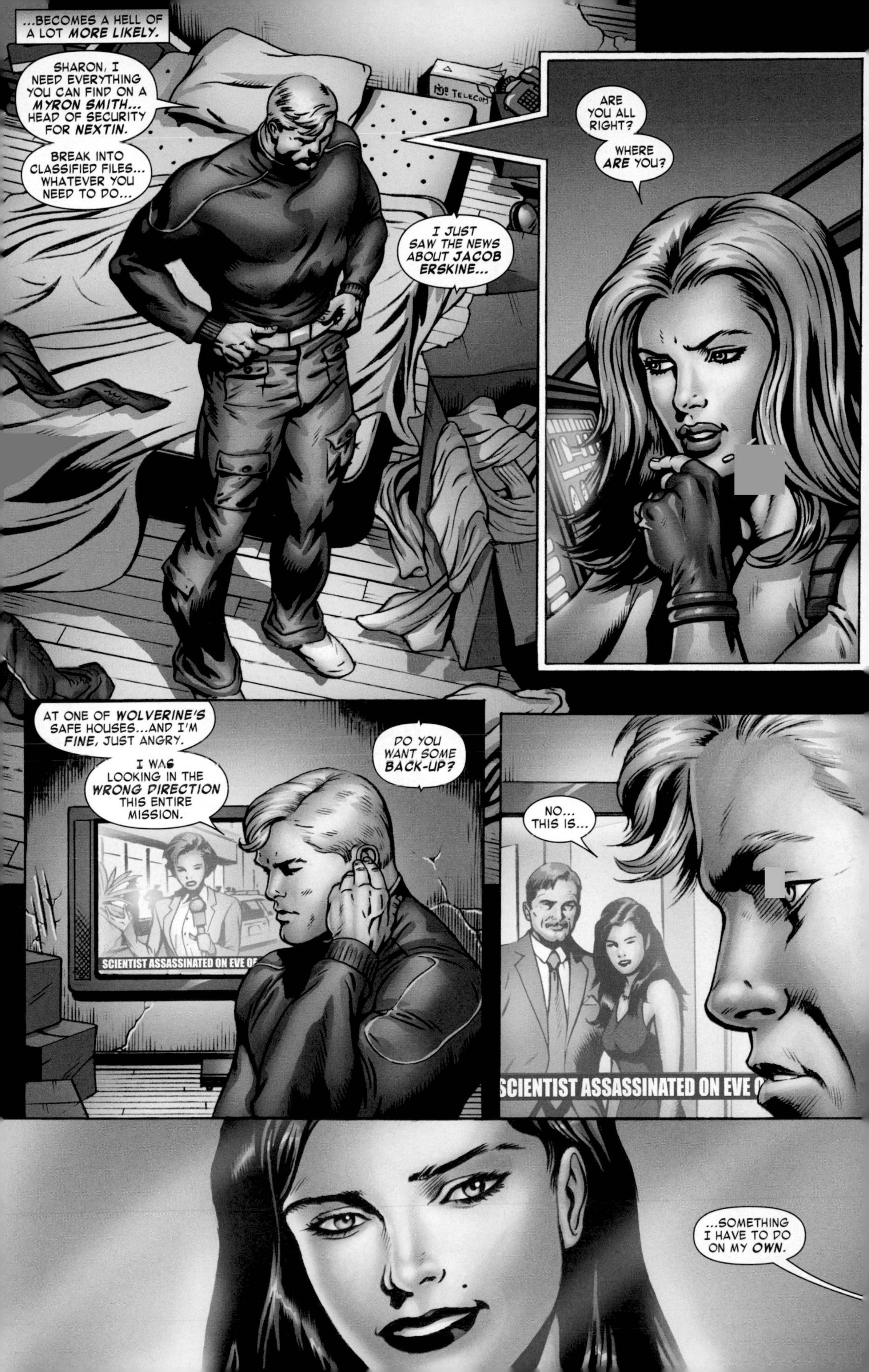
...BECOMES A HELL OF A LOT MORE LIKELY.
SHARON, I NEED EVERYTHING YOU CAN FIND ON A MYRON SMITH... HEAD OF SECURITY FOR NEXTIN.
BREAK INTO CLASSIFIED FILES... WHATEVER YOU NEED TO DO...
I JUST SAW THE NEWS ABOUT JACOB ERSKINE...
ARE YOU ALL RIGHT?
WHERE ARE YOU?
AT ONE OF WOLVERINE'S SAFE HOUSES...AND I'M FINE, JUST ANGRY.
I WAS LOOKING IN THE WRONG DIRECTION THIS ENTIRE MISSION.
DO YOU WANT SOME BACK-UP?
SCIENTIST ASSASSINATED ON EVE OF
NO... THIS IS...
SCIENTIST ASSASSINATED ON EVE O
...SOMETHING I HAVE TO DO ON MY OWN.

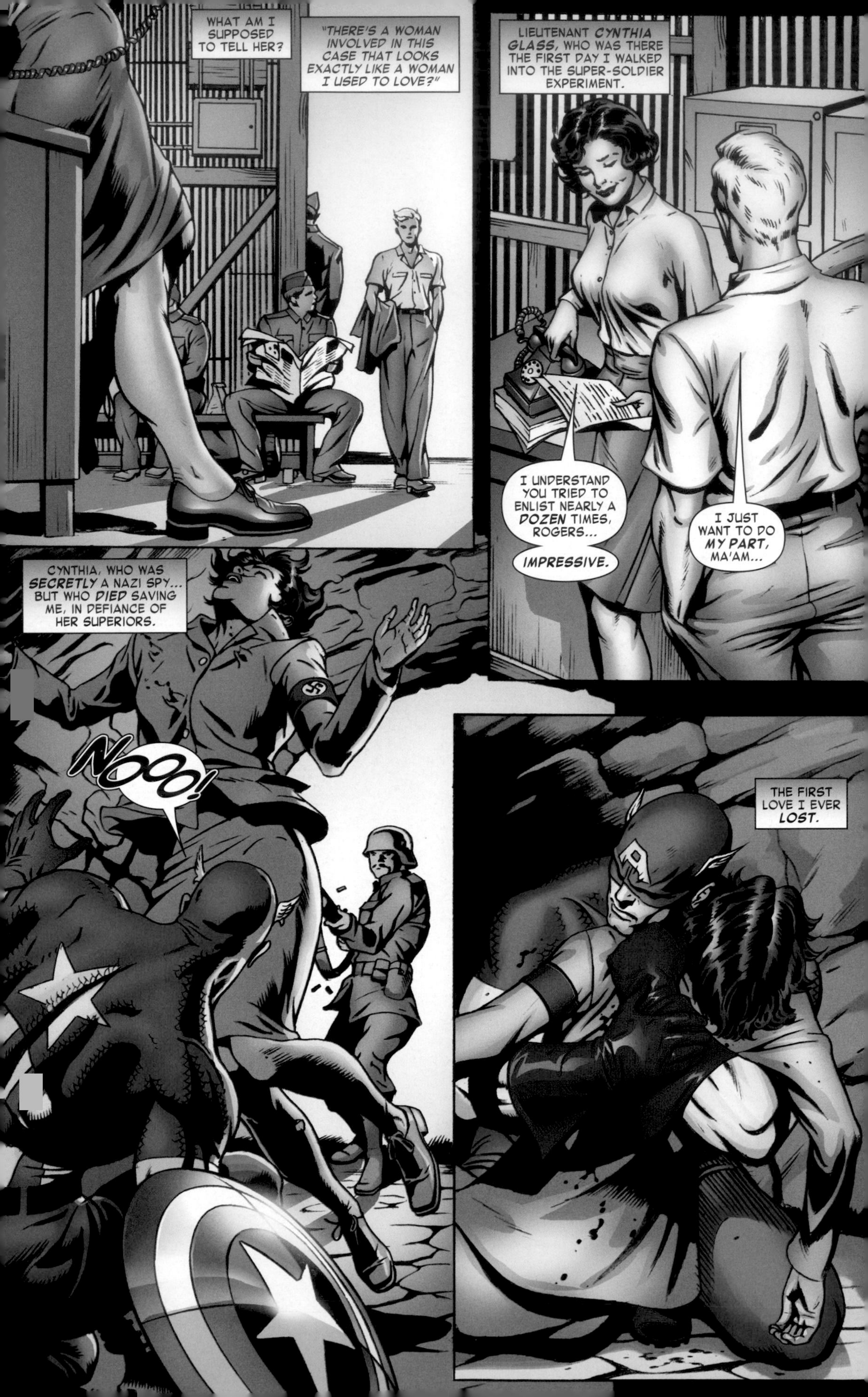
WHAT AM I SUPPOSED TO TELL HER?
"THERE'S A WOMAN INVOLVED IN THIS CASE THAT LOOKS EXACTLY LIKE A WOMAN I USED TO LOVE?"
LIEUTENANT CYNTHIA GLASS, WHO WAS THERE THE FIRST DAY I WALKED INTO THE SUPER-SOLDIER EXPERIMENT.
I UNDERSTAND YOU TRIED TO ENLIST NEARLY A DOZEN TIMES, ROGERS...
IMPRESSIVE.
I JUST WANT TO DO MY PART, MA'AM...
CYNTHIA, WHO WAS SECRETLY A NAZI SPY... BUT WHO DIED SAVING ME, IN DEFIANCE OF HER SUPERIORS.
NOOO!
THE FIRST LOVE I EVER LOST.

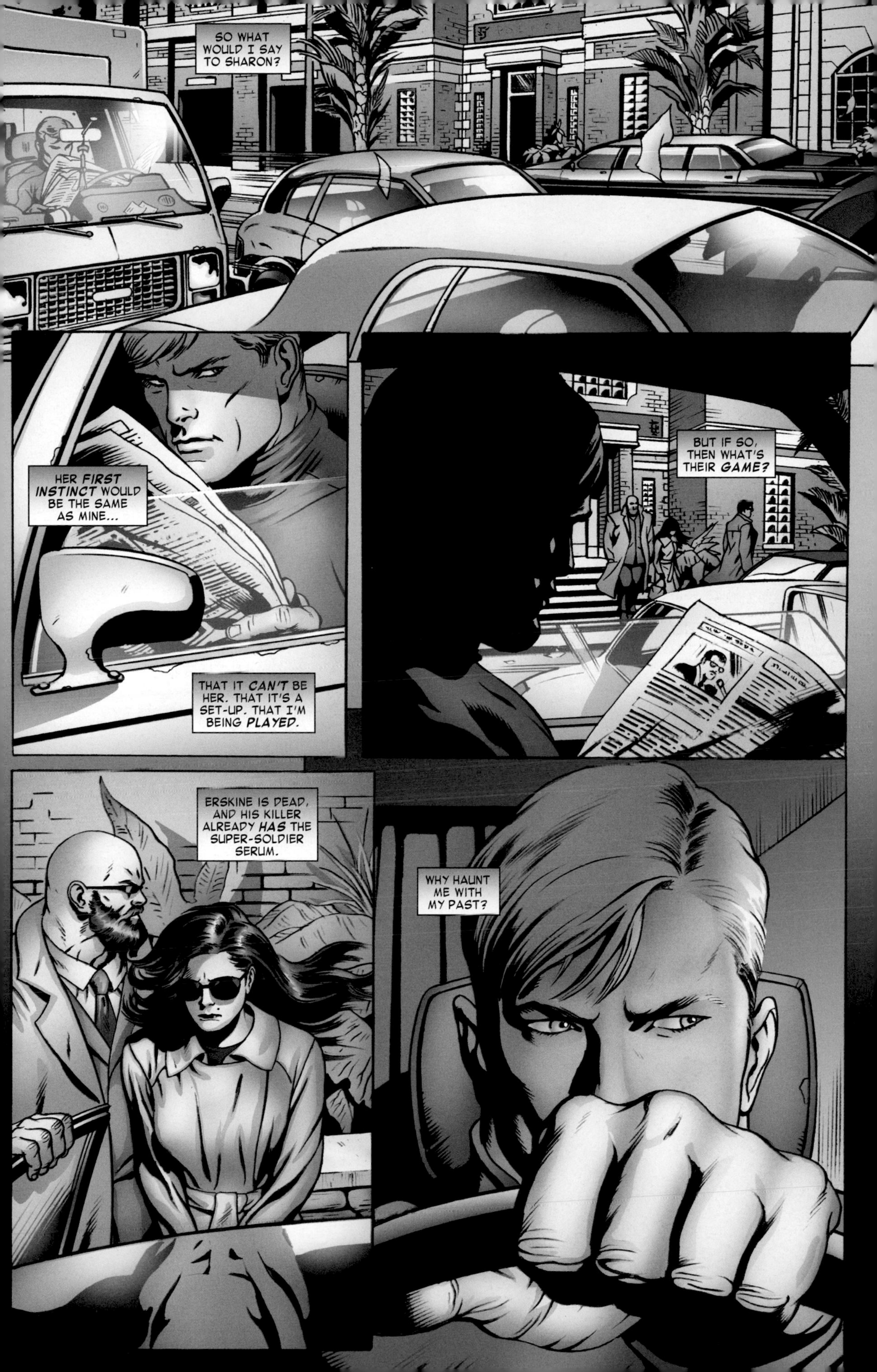
SO WHAT WOULD I SAY TO SHARON?
HER FIRST INSTINCT WOULD BE THE SAME AS MINE...
THAT IT CAN'T BE HER. THAT IT'S A SET-UP. THAT I'M BEING PLAYED.
BUT IF SO, THEN WHAT'S THEIR GAME?
ERSKINE IS DEAD, AND HIS KILLER ALREADY HAS THE SUPER-SOLDIER SERUM.
WHY HAUNT ME WITH MY PAST?

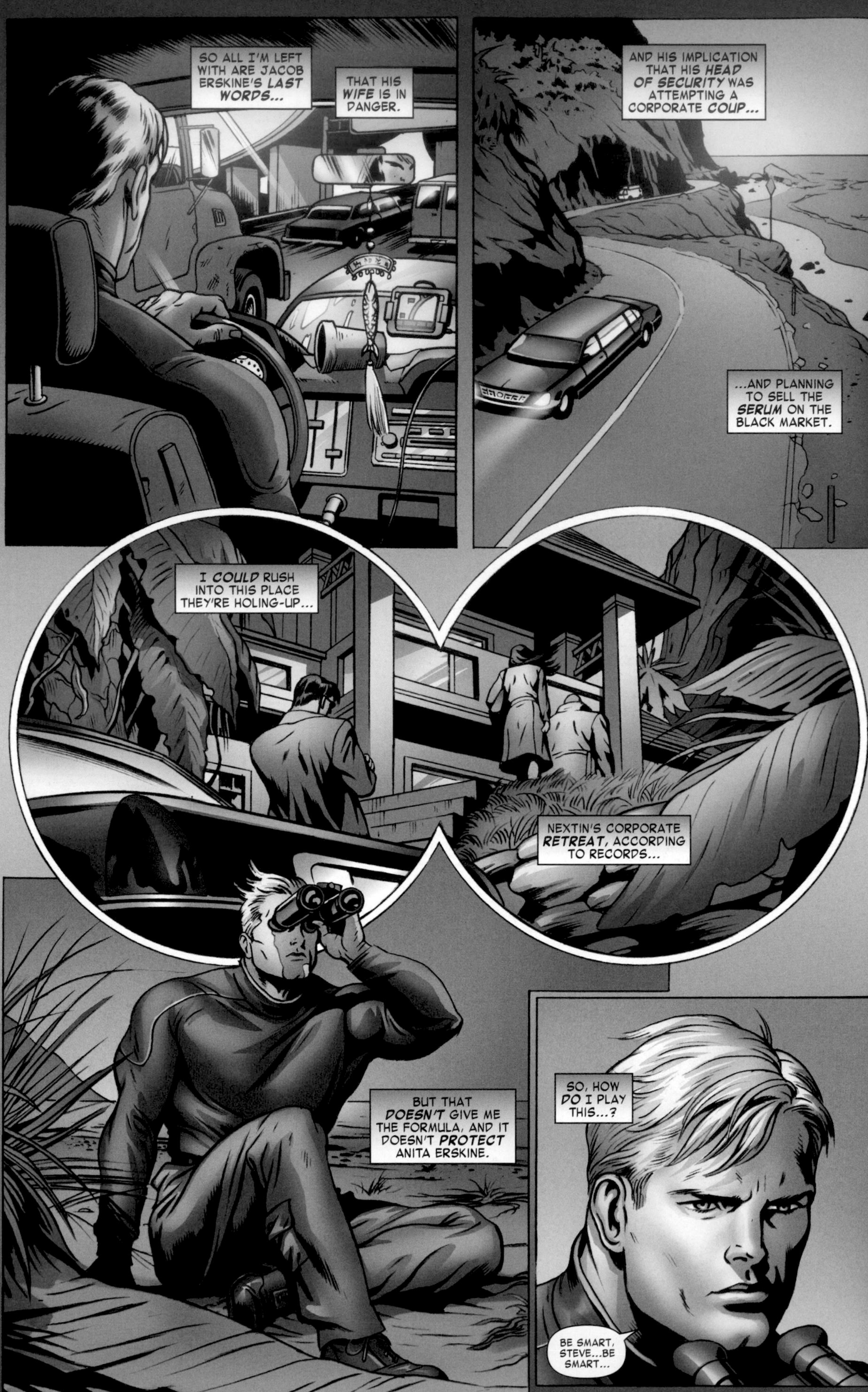
SO ALL I'M LEFT WITH ARE JACOB ERSKINE'S LAST WORDS...
THAT HIS WIFE IS IN DANGER.
AND HIS IMPLICATION THAT HIS HEAD OF SECURITY WAS ATTEMPTING A CORPORATE COUP...
...AND PLANNING TO SELL THE SERUM ON THE BLACK MARKET.
I COULD RUSH INTO THIS PLACE THEY'RE HOLING-UP...
NEXTIN'S CORPORATE RETREAT, ACCORDING TO RECORDS...
BUT THAT DOESN'T GIVE ME THE FORMULA, AND IT DOESN'T PROTECT ANITA ERSKINE.
SO, HOW DO I PLAY THIS...?
BE SMART, STEVE...BE SMART...

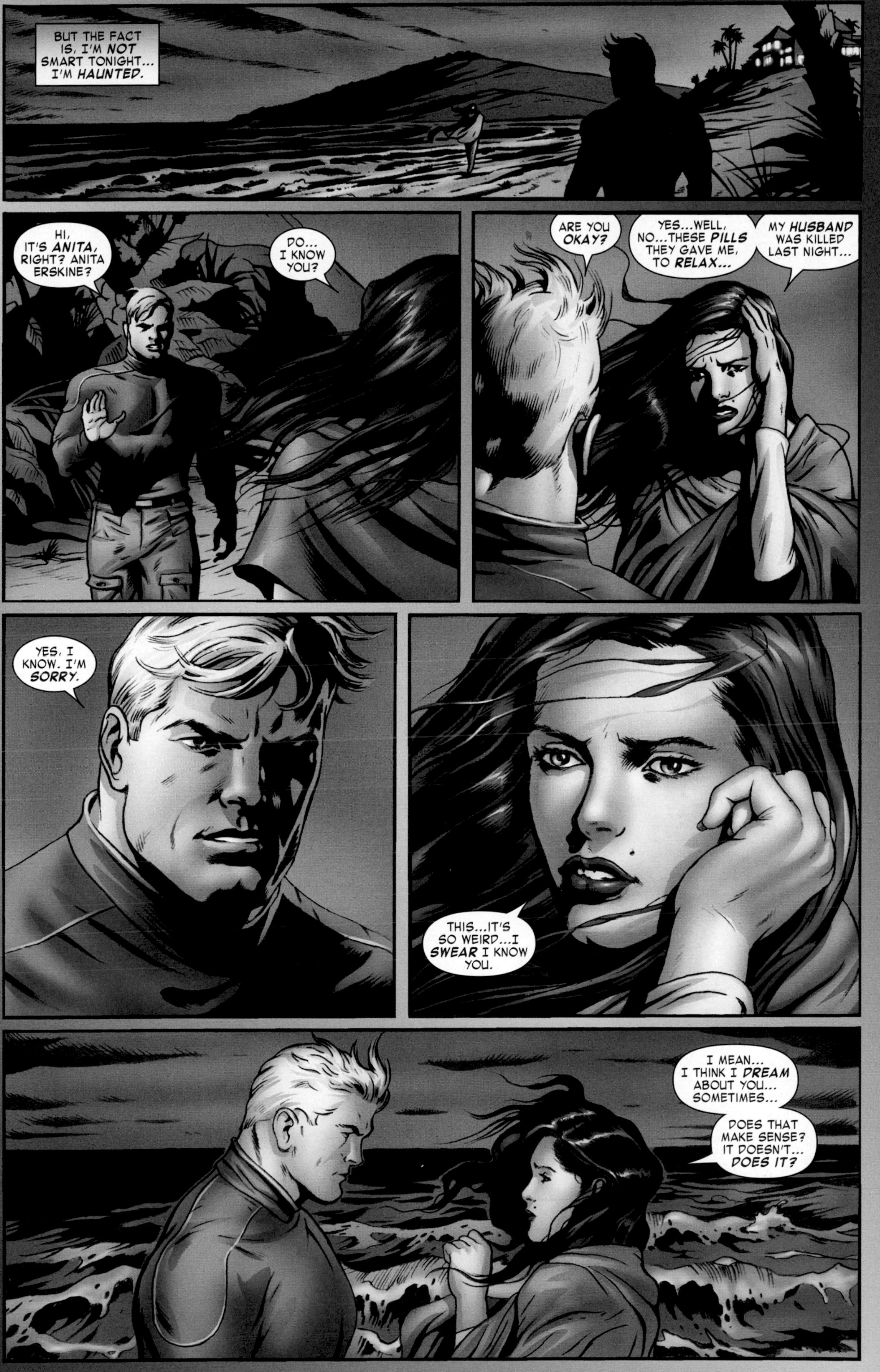

BUT THE FACT IS, I'M NOT SMART TONIGHT... I'M HAUNTED.
HI, IT'S ANITA, RIGHT? ANITA ERSKINE?
DO... I KNOW YOU?
ARE YOU OKAY?
YES...WELL, NO...THESE PILLS THEY GAVE ME, TO RELAX...
MY HUSBAND WAS KILLED LAST NIGHT...
YES, I KNOW. I'M SORRY.
THIS...IT'S SO WEIRD...I SWEAR I KNOW YOU.
I MEAN... I THINK I DREAM ABOUT YOU... SOMETIMES...
DOES THAT MAKE SENSE? IT DOESN'T... DOES IT?

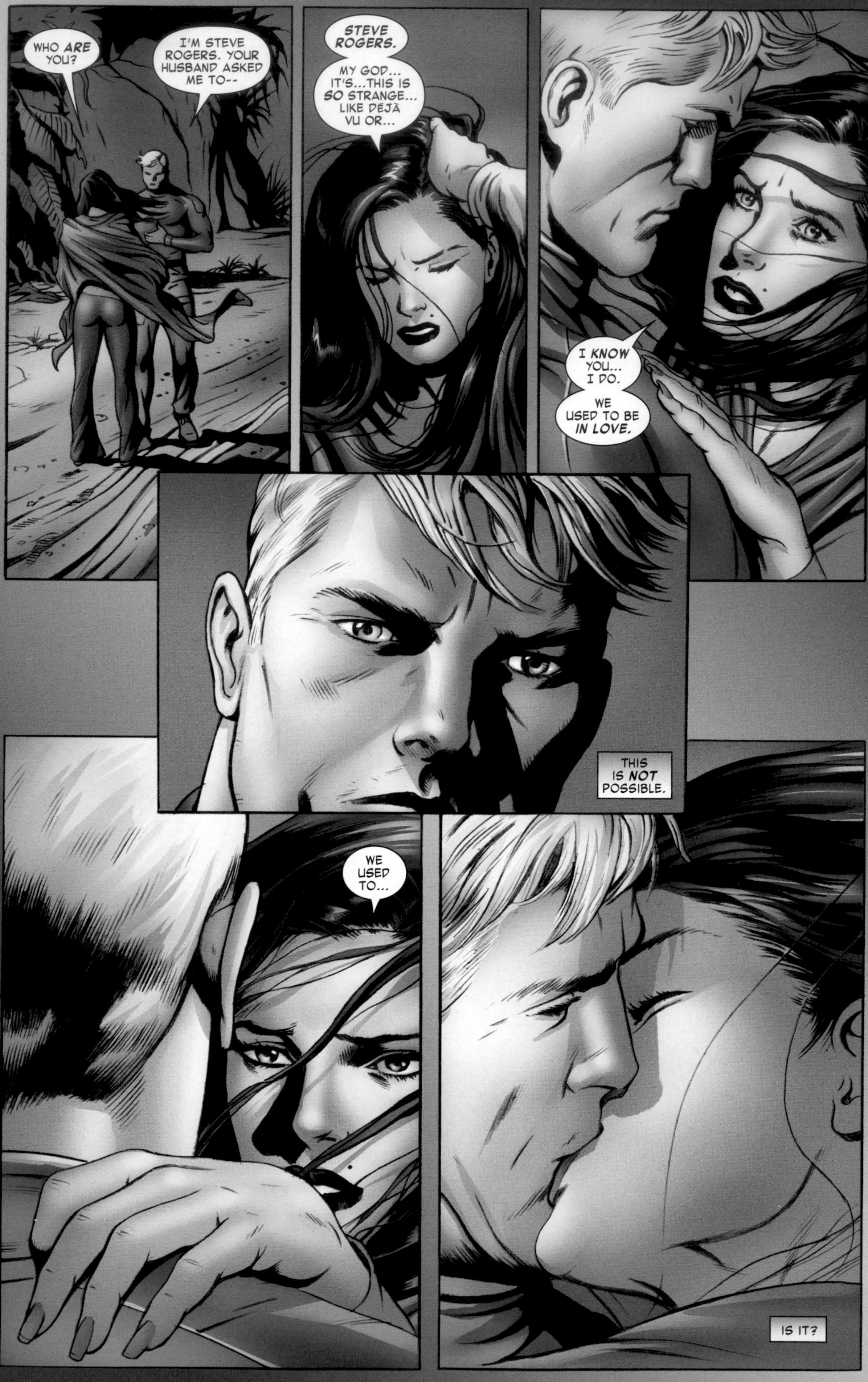
WHO ARE YOU?
I'M STEVE ROGERS. YOUR HUSBAND ASKED ME TO--
STEVE ROGERS.
MY GOD... IT'S...THIS IS SO STRANGE... LIKE DEJÀ VU OR...
I KNOW YOU... I DO.
WE USED TO BE IN LOVE.
THIS IS NOT POSSIBLE.
WE USED TO...
IS IT?

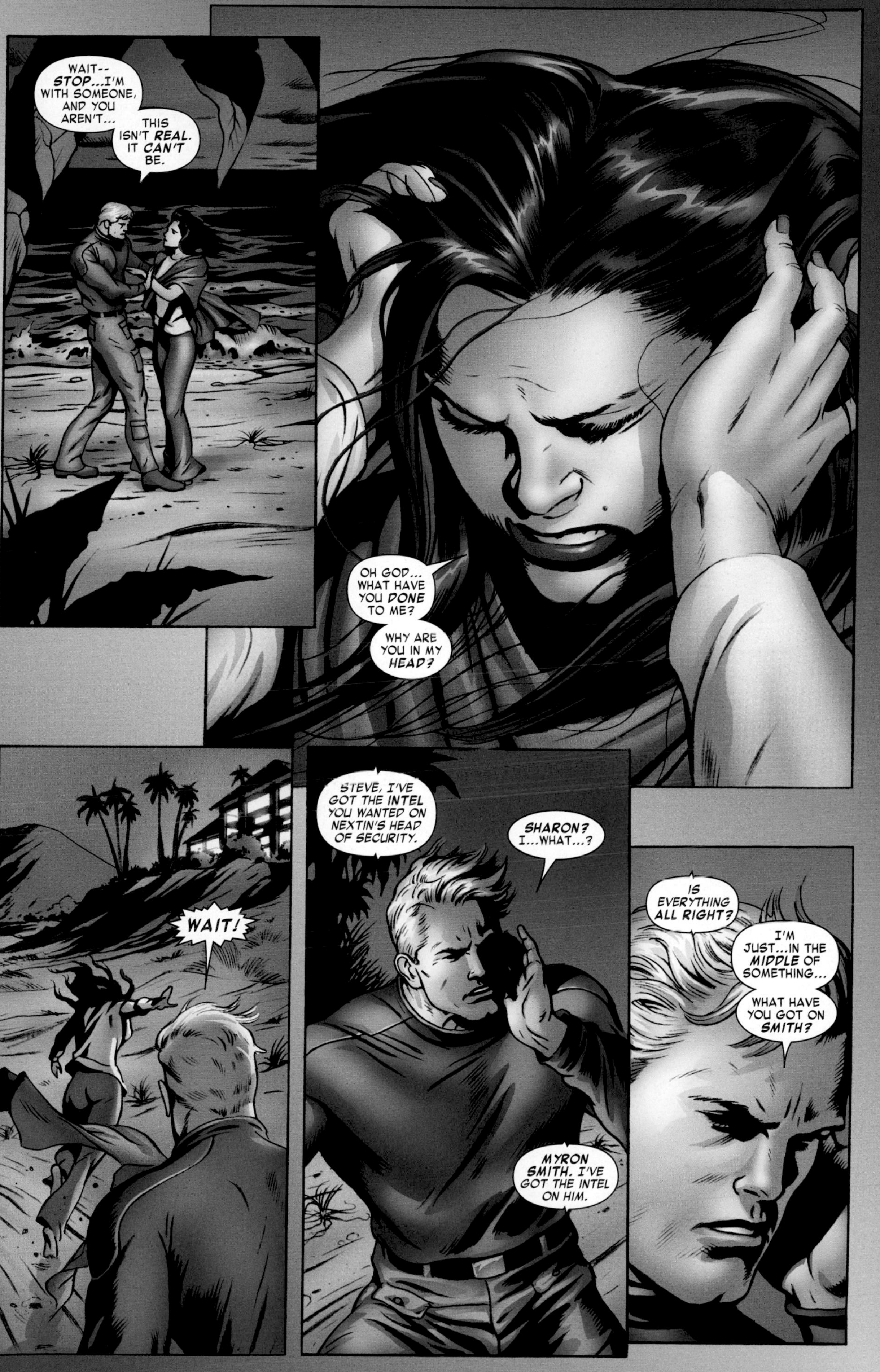
WAIT-- STOP...I'M WITH SOMEONE, AND YOU AREN'T...
THIS ISN'T REAL. IT CAN'T BE.
OH GOD... WHAT HAVE YOU DONE TO ME?
WHY ARE YOU IN MY HEAD?
WAIT!
STEVE, I'VE GOT THE INTEL YOU WANTED ON NEXTIN'S HEAD OF SECURITY.
SHARON? I...WHAT...?
IS EVERYTHING ALL RIGHT?
I'M JUST...IN THE MIDDLE OF SOMETHING...
WHAT HAVE YOU GOT ON SMITH?
MYRON SMITH. I'VE GOT THE INTEL ON HIM.

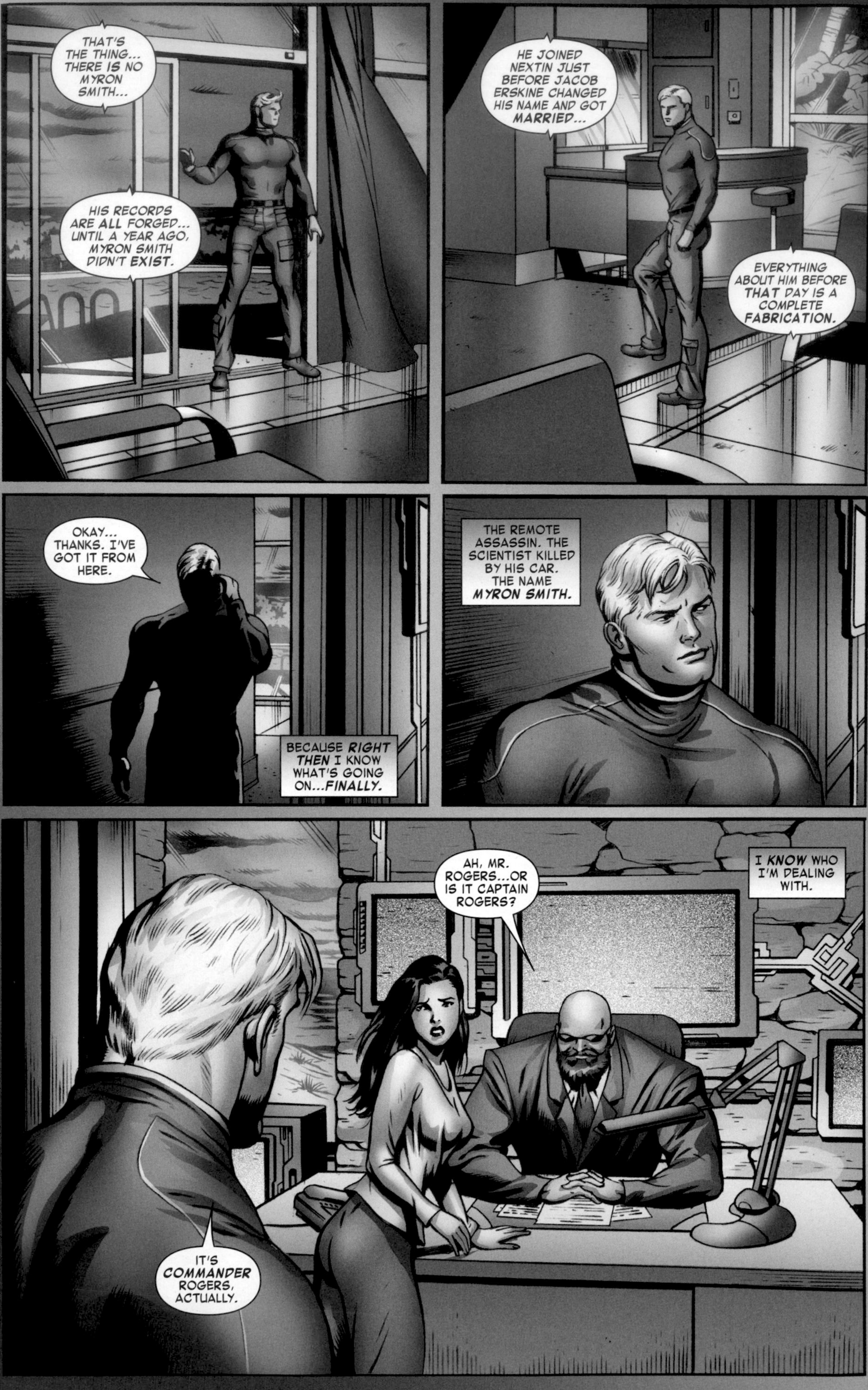
THAT'S THE THING... THERE IS NO MYRON SMITH...
HIS RECORDS ARE ALL FORGED... UNTIL A YEAR AGO, MYRON SMITH DIDN'T EXIST.
HE JOINED NEXTIN JUST BEFORE JACOB ERSKINE CHANGED HIS NAME AND GOT MARRIED...
EVERYTHING ABOUT HIM BEFORE THAT DAY IS A COMPLETE FABRICATION.
OKAY... THANKS. I'VE GOT IT FROM HERE.
BECAUSE RIGHT THEN I KNOW WHAT'S GOING ON...FINALLY.
THE REMOTE ASSASSIN. THE SCIENTIST KILLED BY HIS CAR. THE NAME MYRON SMITH.
AH, MR. ROGERS...OR IS IT CAPTAIN ROGERS?
I KNOW WHO I'M DEALING WITH.
IT'S COMMANDER ROGERS, ACTUALLY.

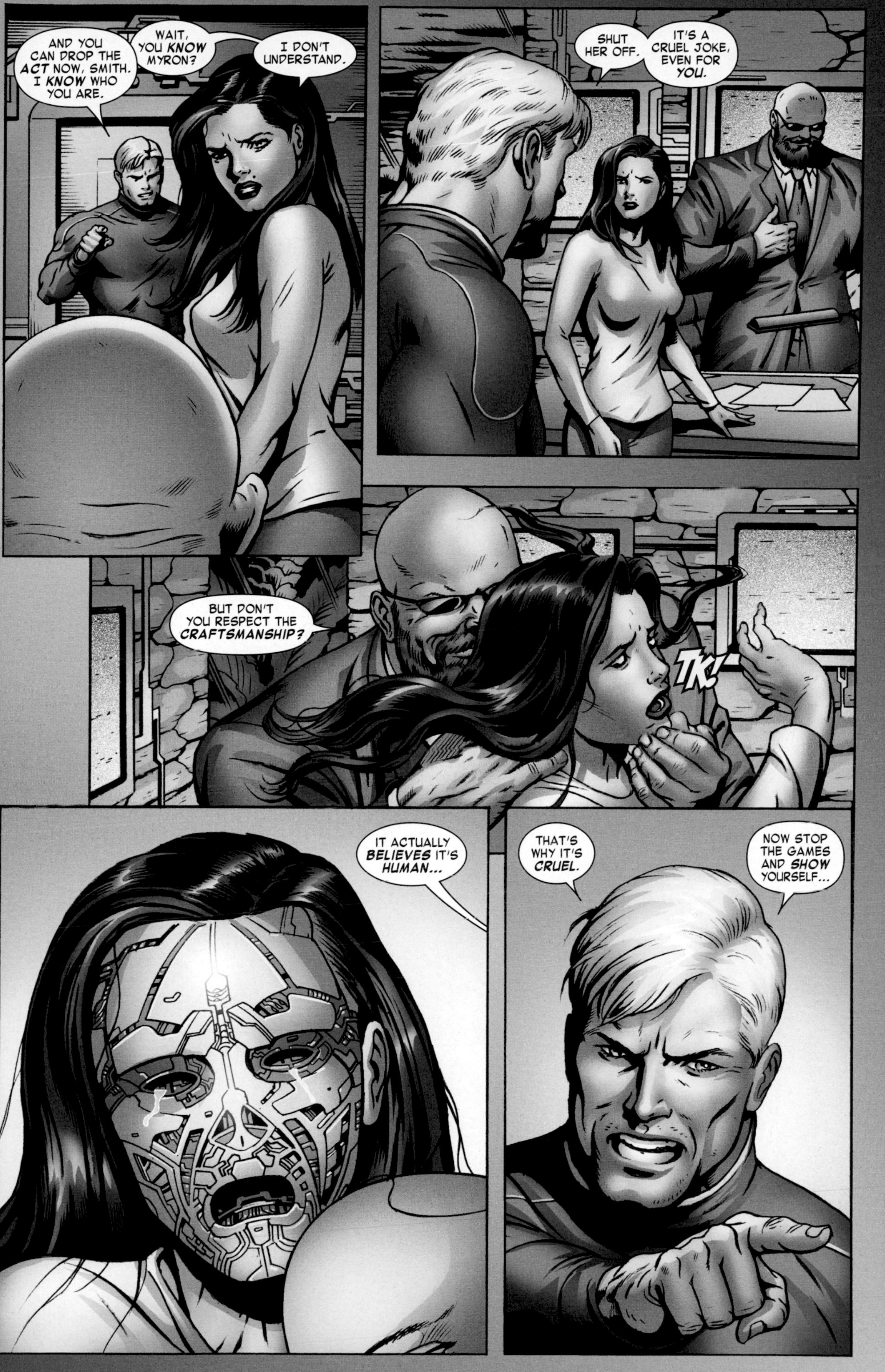
AND YOU CAN DROP THE ACT NOW, SMITH. I KNOW WHO YOU ARE.
WAIT, YOU KNOW MYRON?
I DON'T UNDERSTAND.
SHUT HER OFF.
IT'S A CRUEL JOKE, EVEN FOR YOU.
BUT DON'T YOU RESPECT THE CRAFTSMANSHIP?
TK!
IT ACTUALLY BELIEVES IT'S HUMAN...
THAT'S WHY IT'S CRUEL.
NOW STOP THE GAMES AND SHOW YOURSELF...

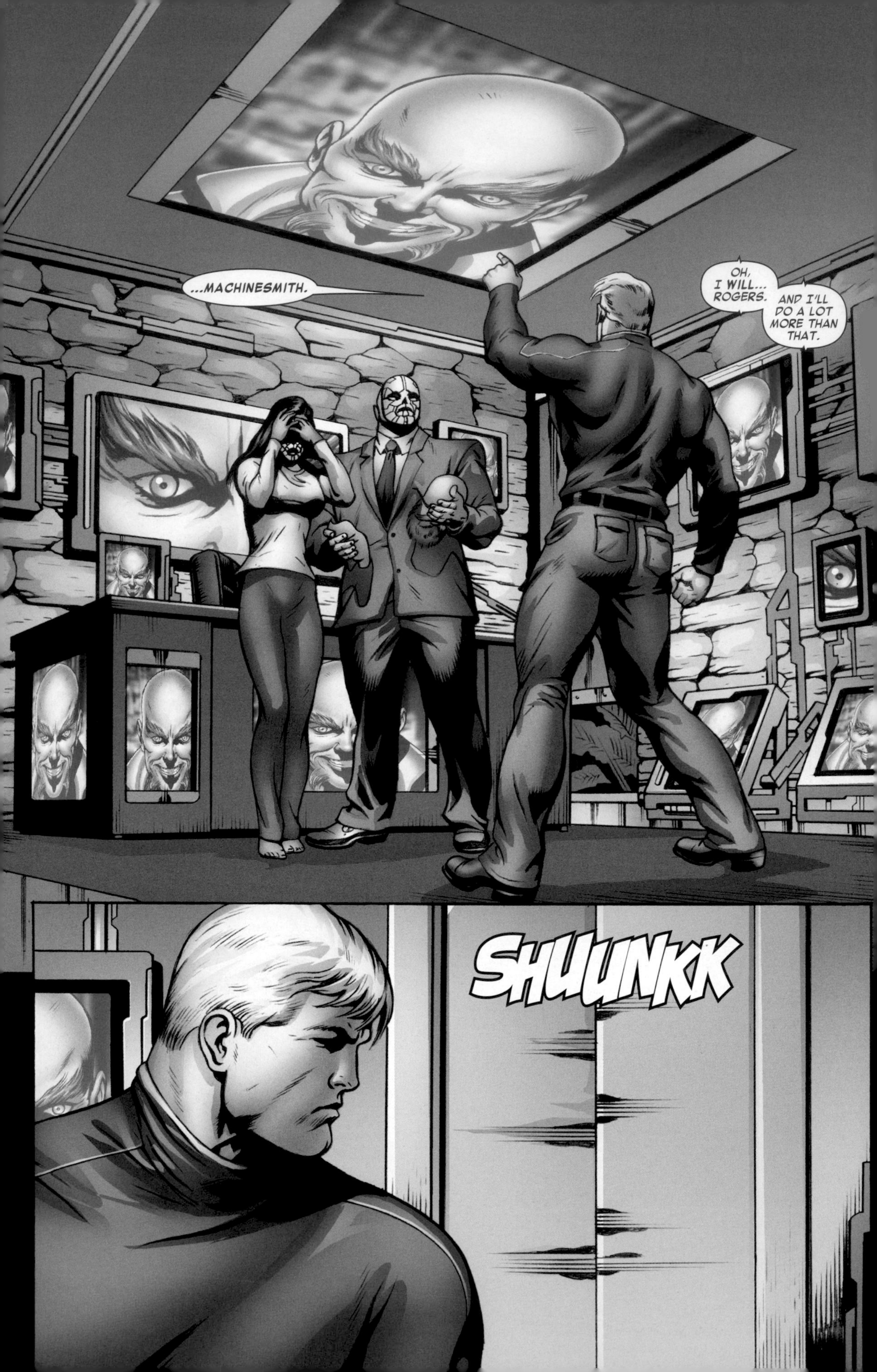
...MACHINESMITH.
OH, I WILL... ROGERS.
AND I'LL DO A LOT MORE THAN THAT.
SHUUNKK

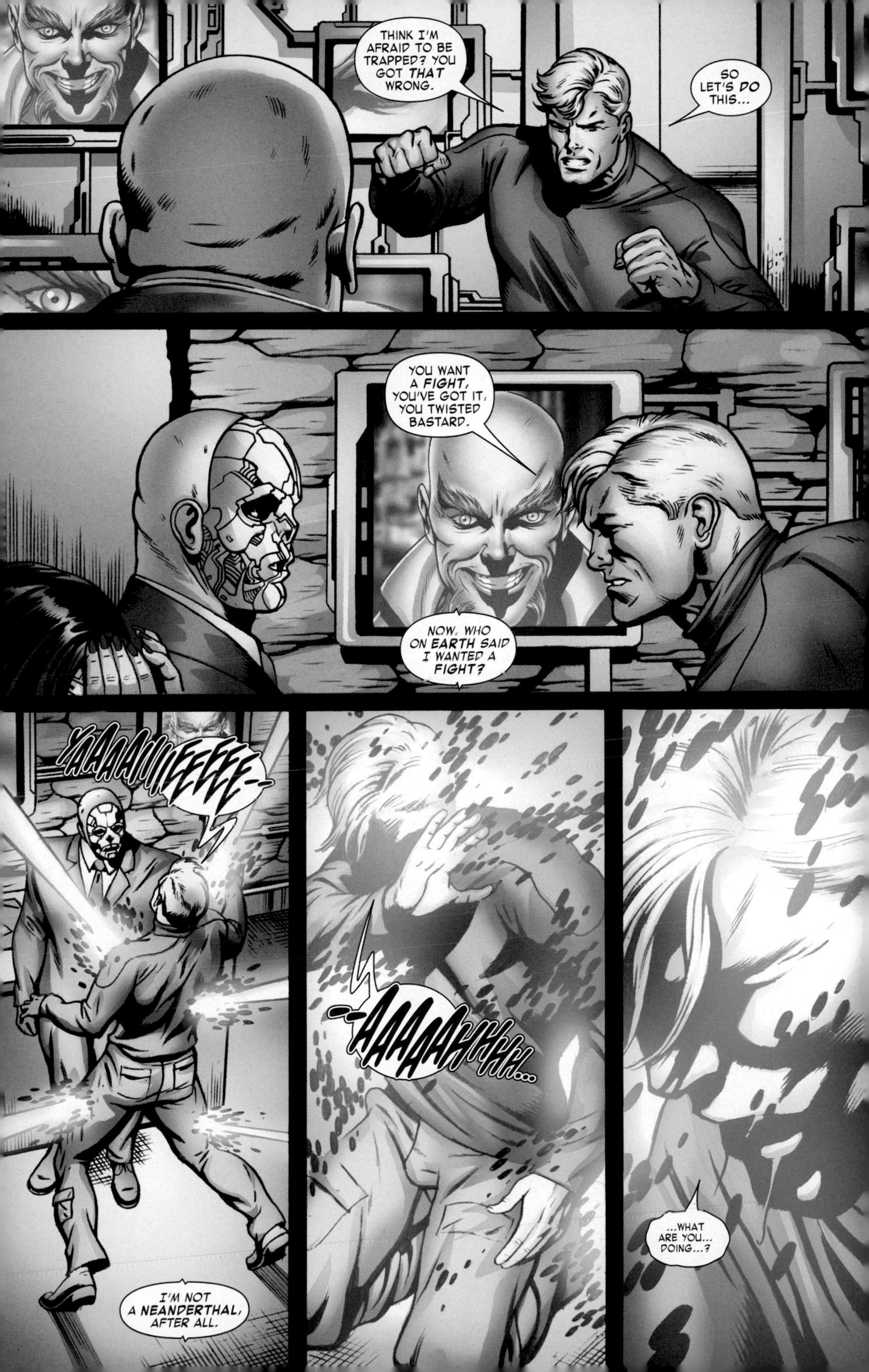
THINK I'M AFRAID TO BE TRAPPED? YOU GOT THAT WRONG.
SO LET'S DO THIS...
YOU WANT A FIGHT, YOU'VE GOT IT, YOU TWISTED BASTARD.
NOW, WHO ON EARTH SAID I WANTED A FIGHT?
YAAAAIIIIEEEEE--
I'M NOT A NEANDERTHAL, AFTER ALL.
--AAAAAHHHH...
...WHAT ARE YOU... DOING...?

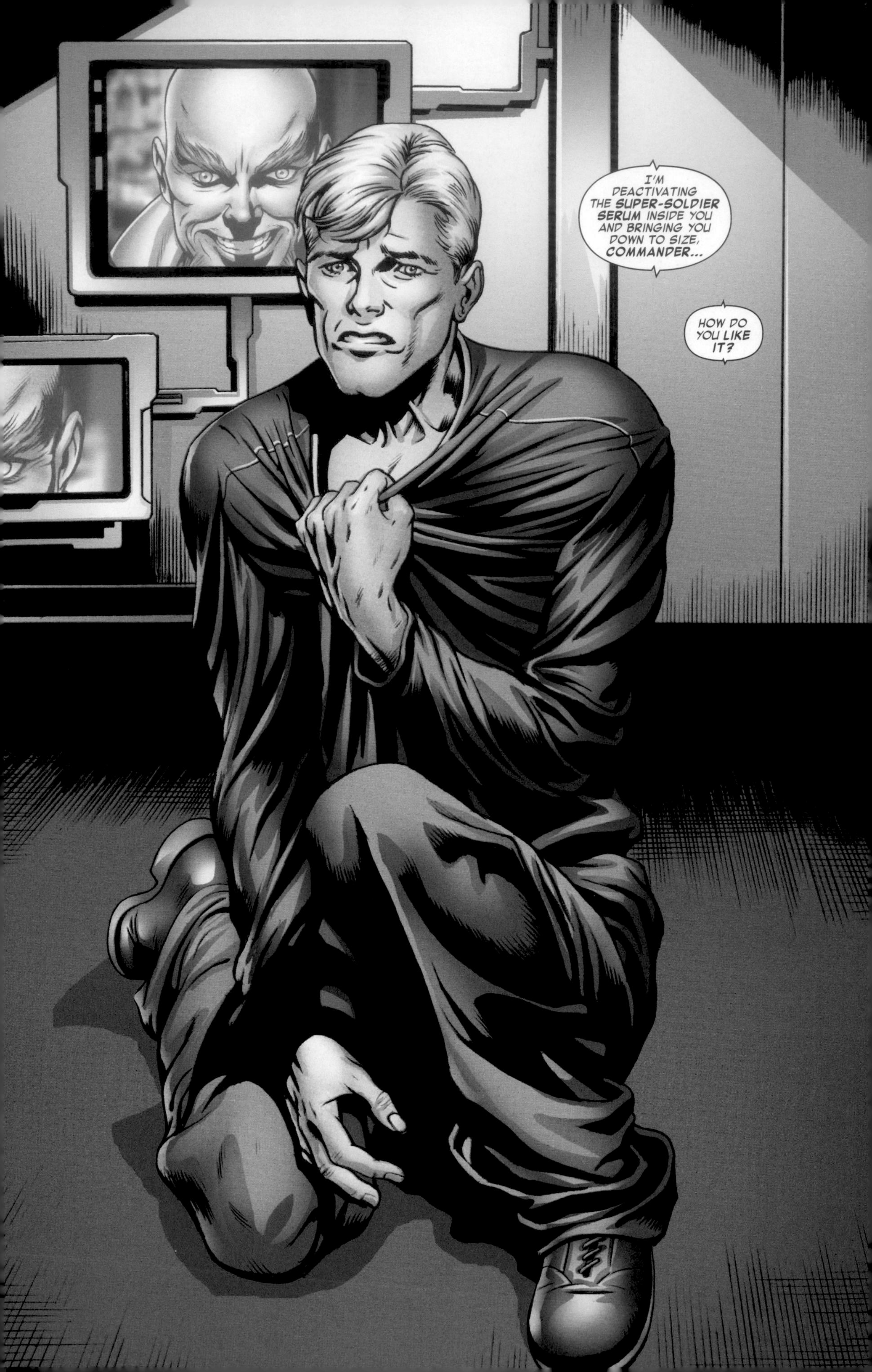
I'M DEACTIVATING THE SUPER-SOLDIER SERUM INSIDE YOU AND BRINGING YOU DOWN TO SIZE, COMMANDER...
HOW DO YOU LIKE IT?

3

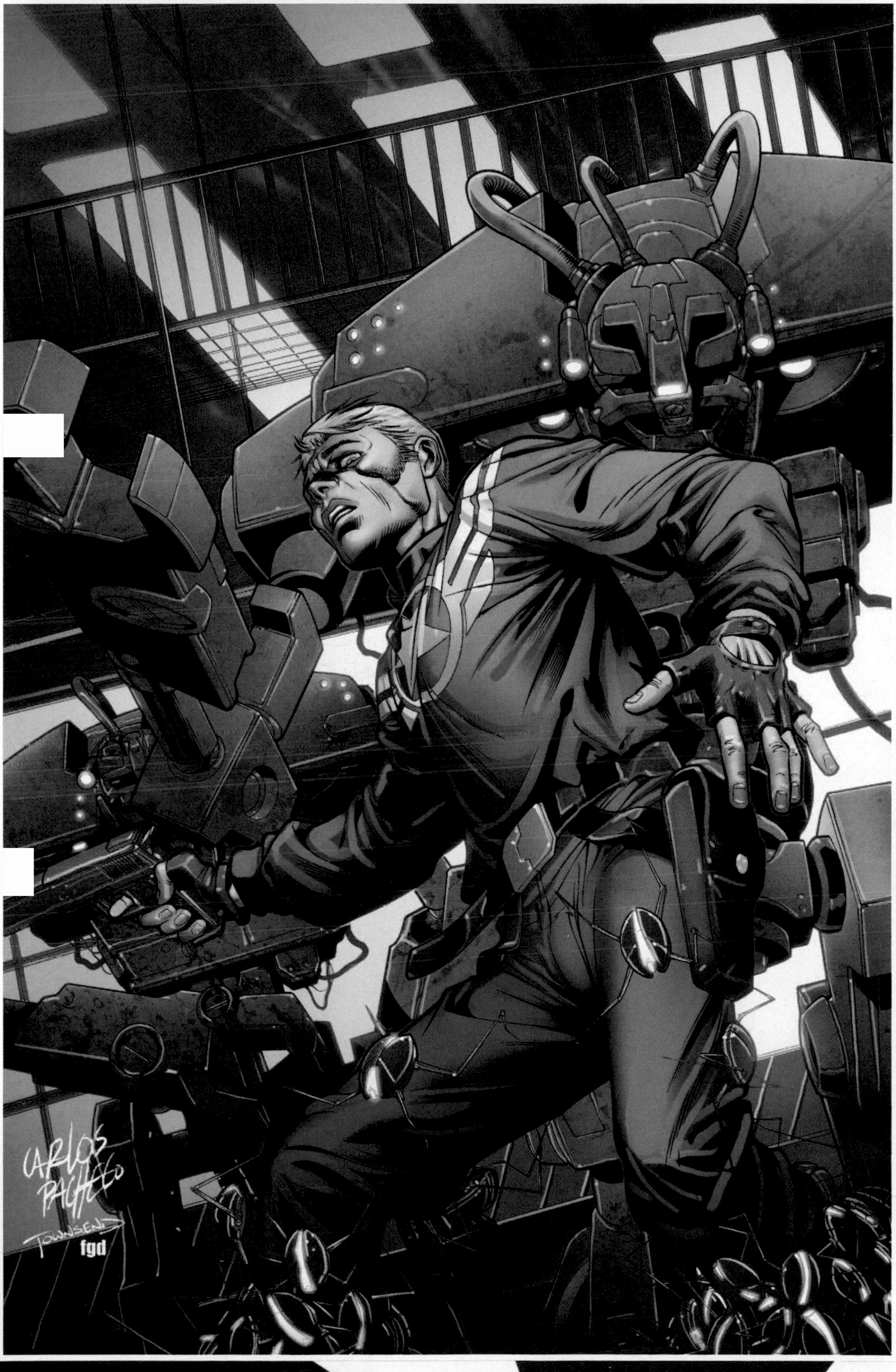
CARLOS PACHECO
TOWNSEND
fgd

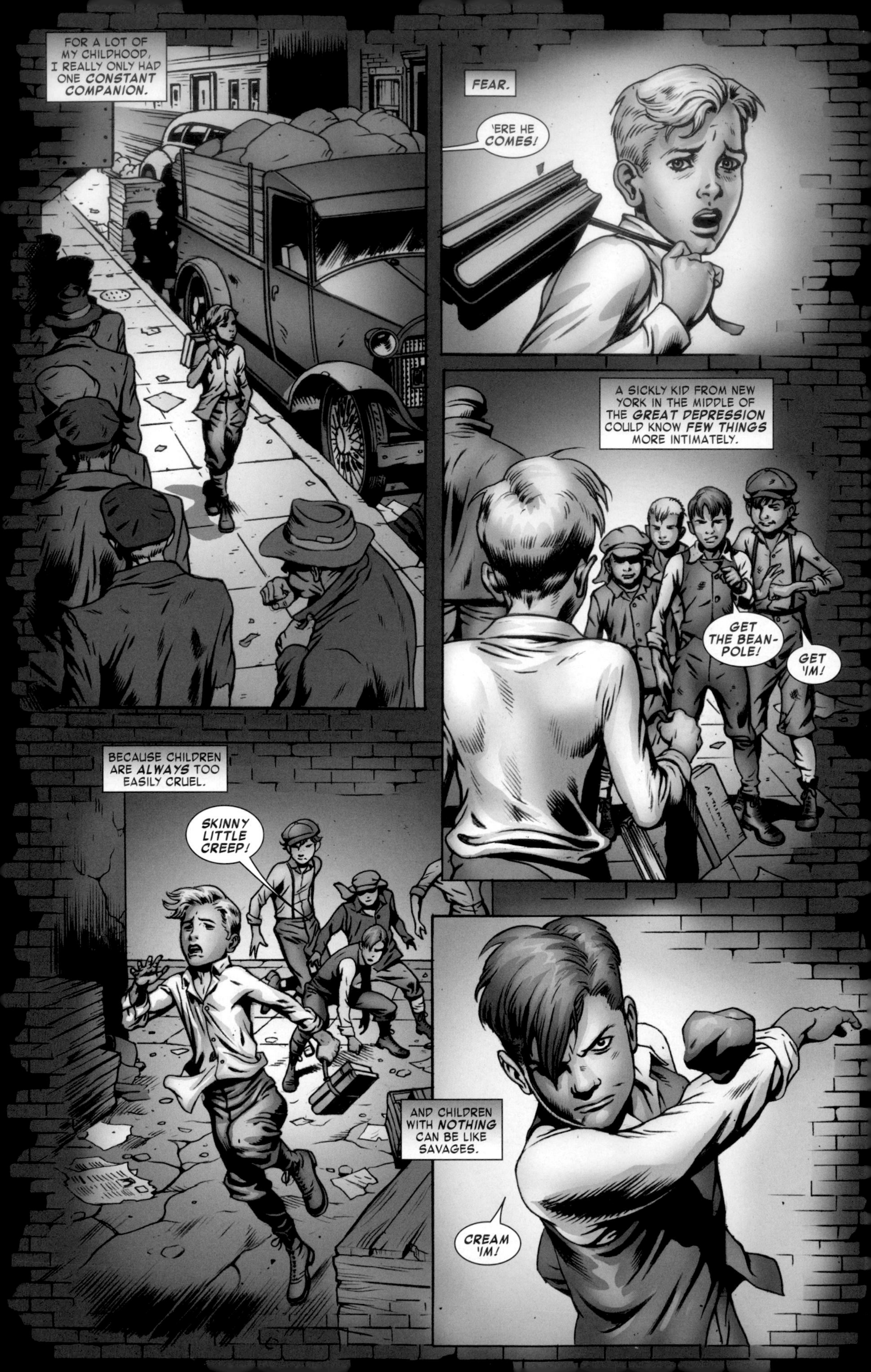
FOR A LOT OF MY CHILDHOOD, I REALLY ONLY HAD ONE CONSTANT COMPANION.
FEAR.
'ERE HE COMES!
A SICKLY KID FROM NEW YORK IN THE MIDDLE OF THE GREAT DEPRESSION COULD KNOW FEW THINGS MORE INTIMATELY.
GET THE BEAN-POLE!
GET 'IM!
BECAUSE CHILDREN ARE ALWAYS TOO EASILY CRUEL.
SKINNY LITTLE CREEP!
AND CHILDREN WITH NOTHING CAN BE LIKE SAVAGES.
CREAM 'IM!

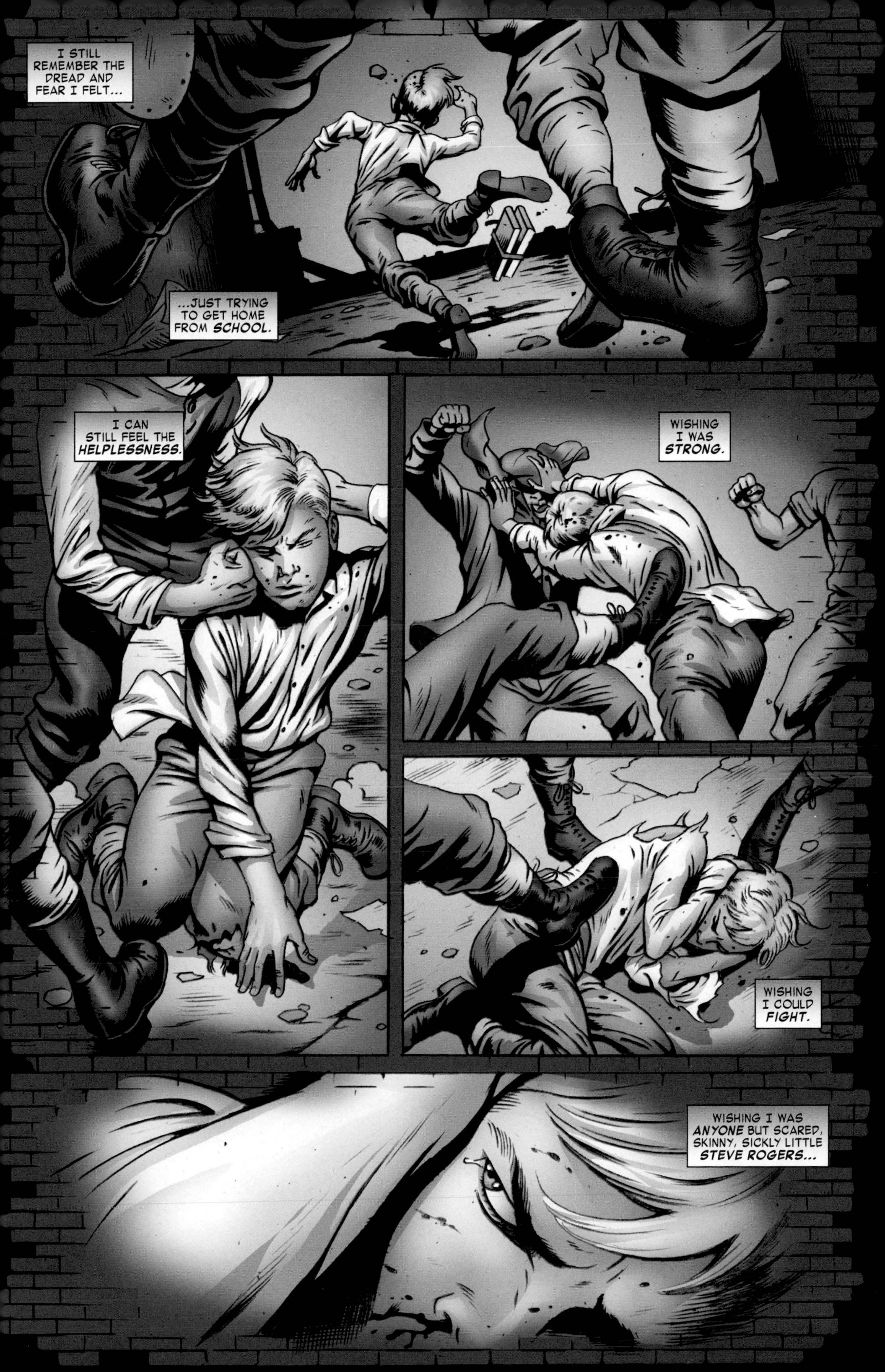
I STILL REMEMBER THE DREAD AND FEAR I FELT...
...JUST TRYING TO GET HOME FROM SCHOOL.
I CAN STILL FEEL THE HELPLESSNESS.
WISHING I WAS STRONG.
WISHING I COULD FIGHT.
WISHING I WAS ANYONE BUT SCARED, SKINNY, SICKLY LITTLE STEVE ROGERS...

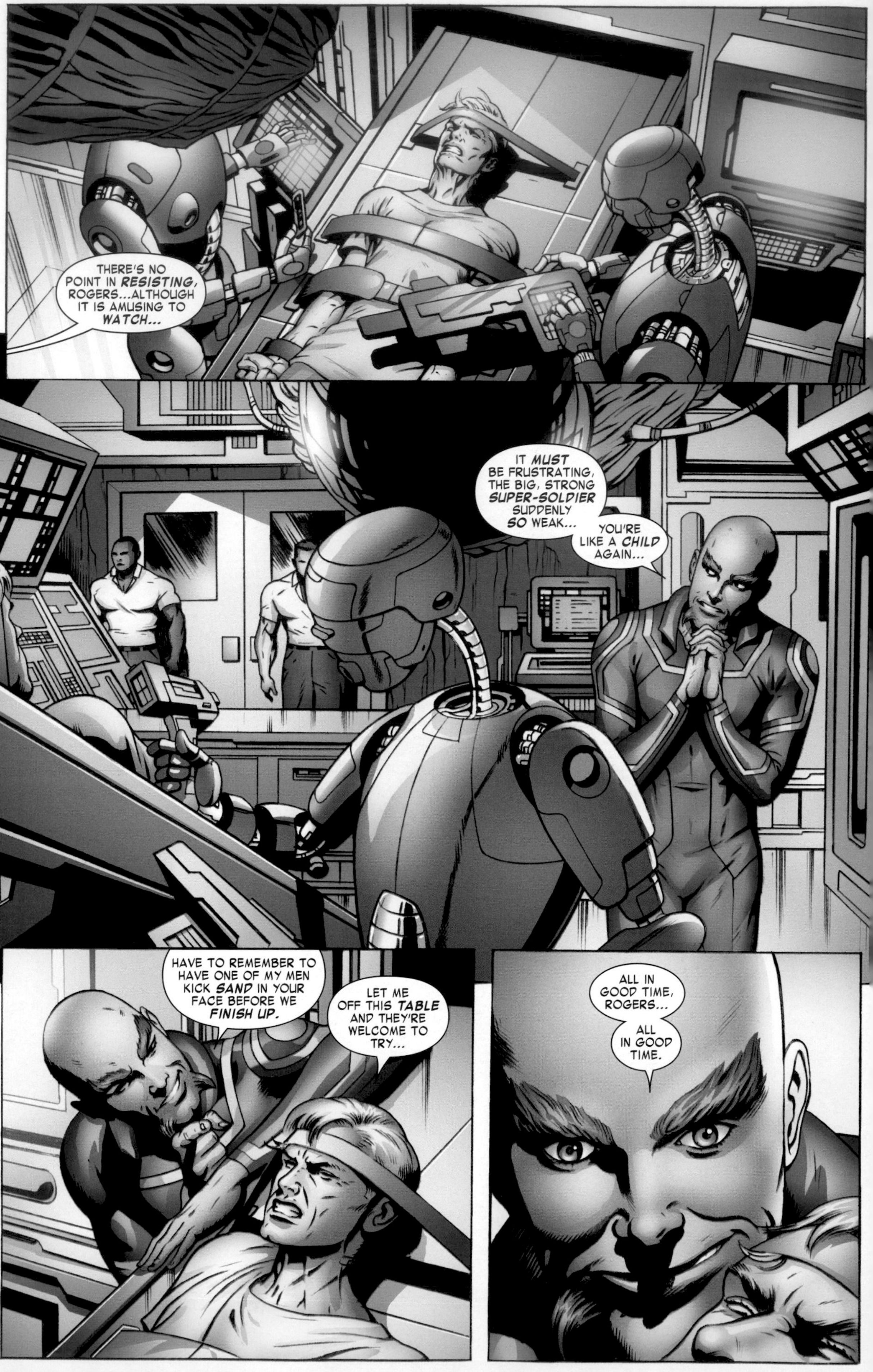
THERE'S NO POINT IN RESISTING, ROGERS...ALTHOUGH IT IS AMUSING TO WATCH...
IT MUST BE FRUSTRATING, THE BIG, STRONG SUPER-SOLDIER SUDDENLY SO WEAK...
YOU'RE LIKE A CHILD AGAIN...
HAVE TO REMEMBER TO HAVE ONE OF MY MEN KICK SAND IN YOUR FACE BEFORE WE FINISH UP.
LET ME OFF THIS TABLE AND THEY'RE WELCOME TO TRY...
ALL IN GOOD TIME, ROGERS...
ALL IN GOOD TIME.

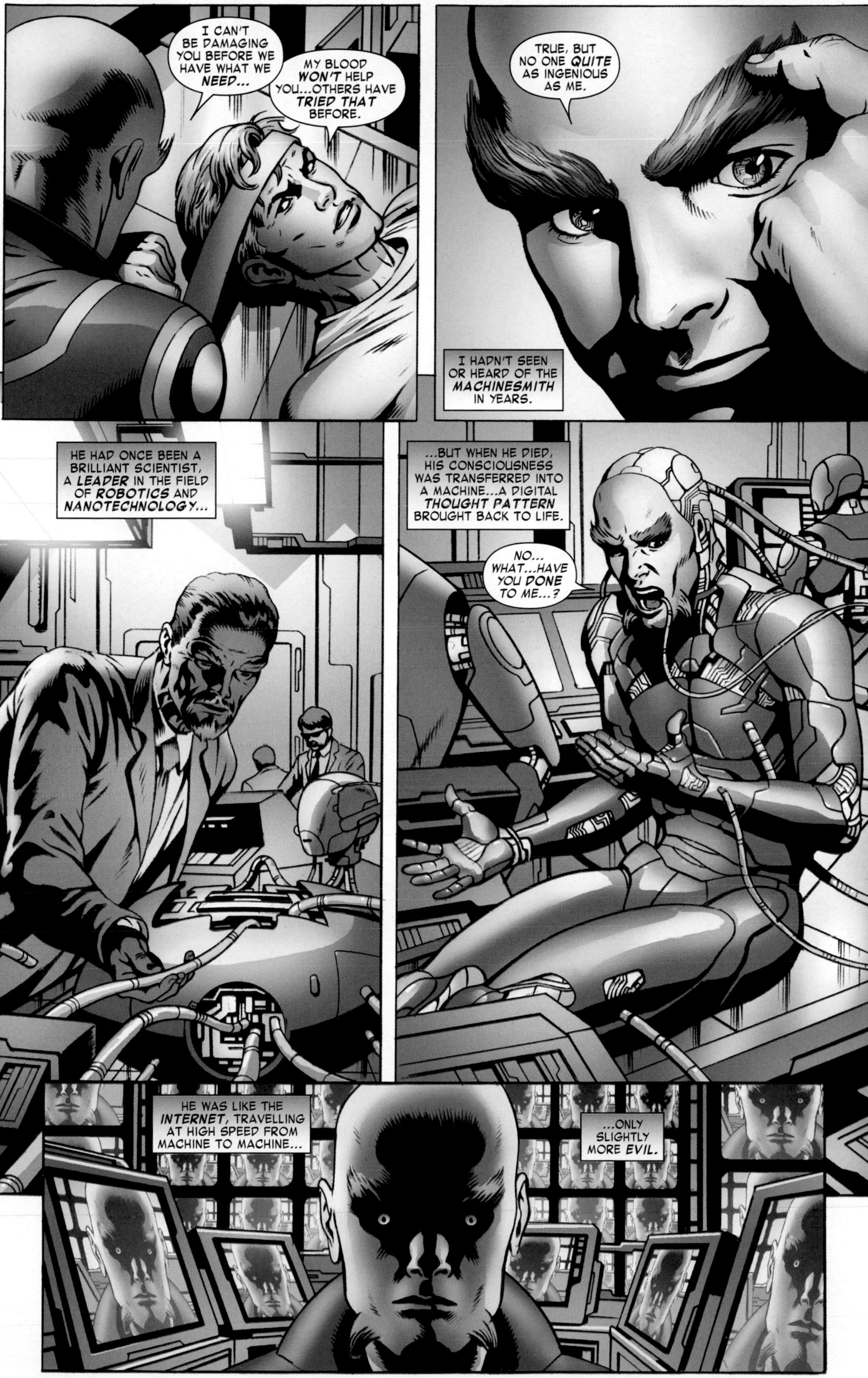
I CAN'T BE DAMAGING YOU BEFORE WE HAVE WHAT WE NEED...
MY BLOOD WON'T HELP YOU...OTHERS HAVE TRIED THAT BEFORE.
TRUE, BUT NO ONE QUITE AS INGENIOUS AS ME.
I HADN'T SEEN OR HEARD OF THE MACHINESMITH IN YEARS.
HE HAD ONCE BEEN A BRILLIANT SCIENTIST, A LEADER IN THE FIELD OF ROBOTICS AND NANOTECHNOLOGY...
...BUT WHEN HE DIED, HIS CONSCIOUSNESS WAS TRANSFERRED INTO A MACHINE...A DIGITAL THOUGHT PATTERN BROUGHT BACK TO LIFE.
NO... WHAT...HAVE YOU DONE TO ME...?
HE WAS LIKE THE INTERNET, TRAVELLING AT HIGH SPEED FROM MACHINE TO MACHINE...
...ONLY SLIGHTLY MORE EVIL.

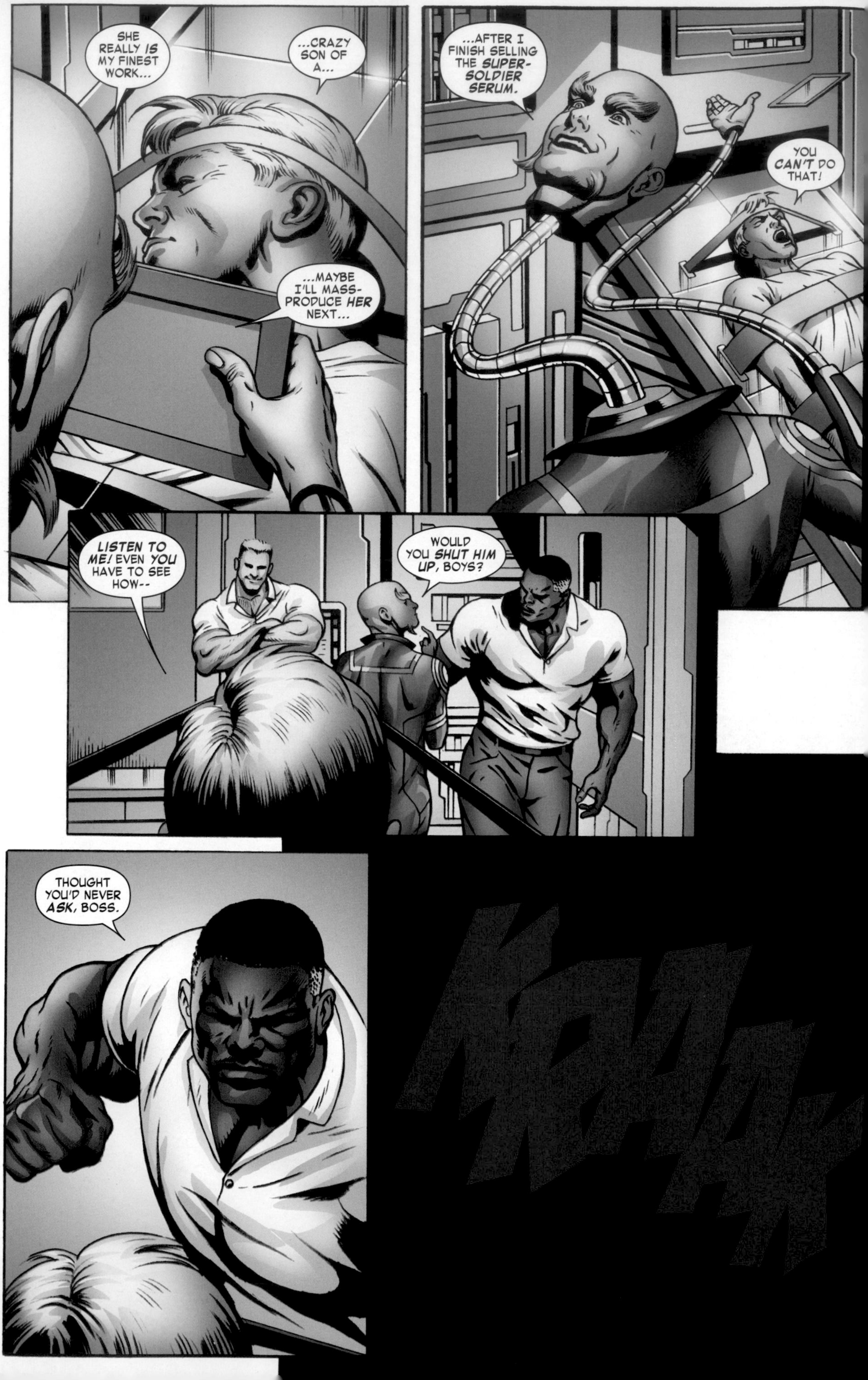
SHE REALLY IS MY FINEST WORK...
...CRAZY SON OF A...
...MAYBE I'LL MASS-PRODUCE HER NEXT...
...AFTER I FINISH SELLING THE SUPER-SOLDIER SERUM.
YOU CAN'T DO THAT!
LISTEN TO ME! EVEN YOU HAVE TO SEE HOW--
WOULD YOU SHUT HIM UP, BOYS?
THOUGHT YOU'D NEVER ASK, BOSS.
KRAAAK

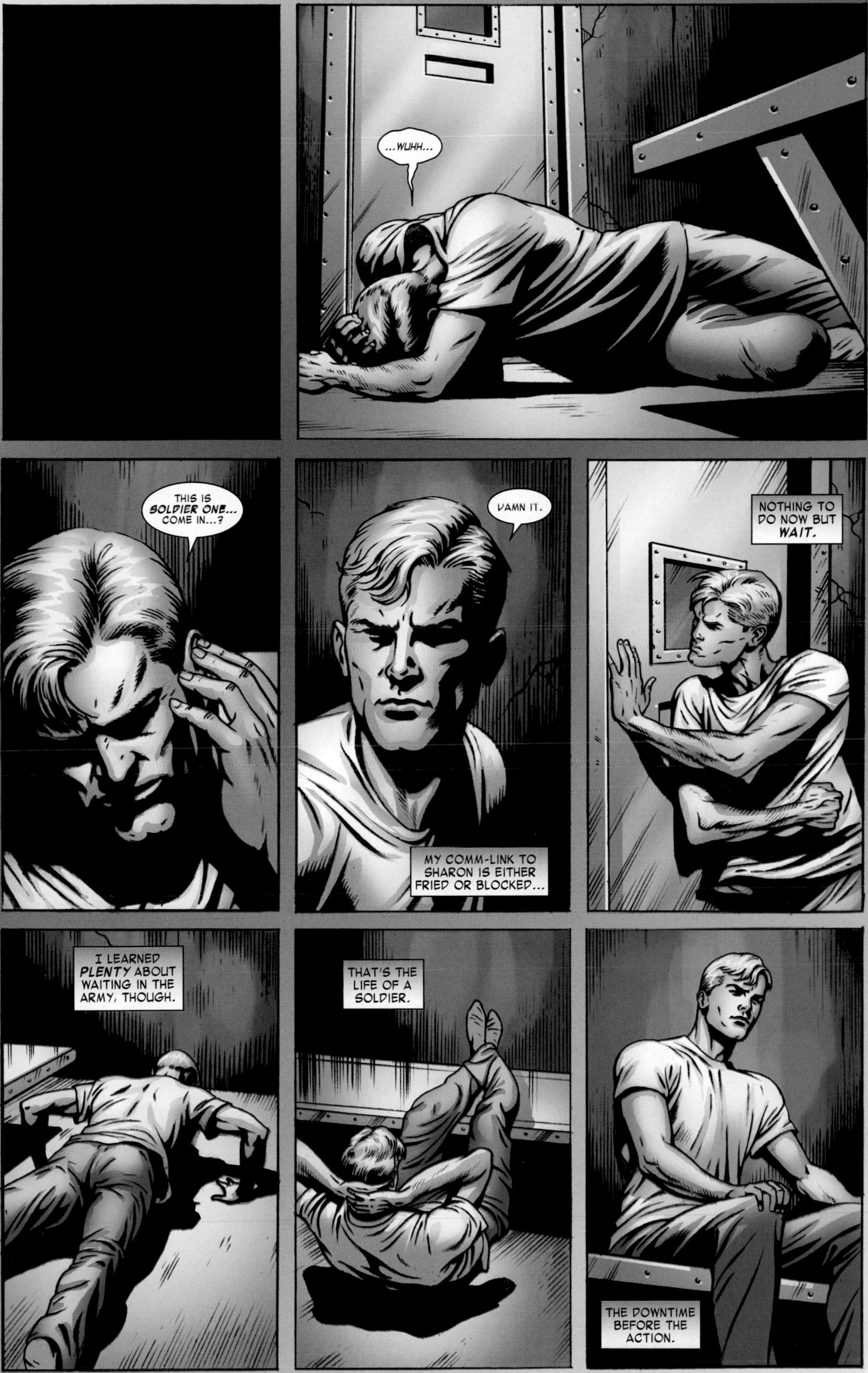
...WUHH...
THIS IS SOLDIER ONE... COME IN...?
DAMN IT.
MY COMM-LINK TO SHARON IS EITHER FRIED OR BLOCKED...
NOTHING TO DO NOW BUT WAIT.
I LEARNED PLENTY ABOUT WAITING IN THE ARMY, THOUGH.
THAT'S THE LIFE OF A SOLDIER.
THE DOWNTIME BEFORE THE ACTION.

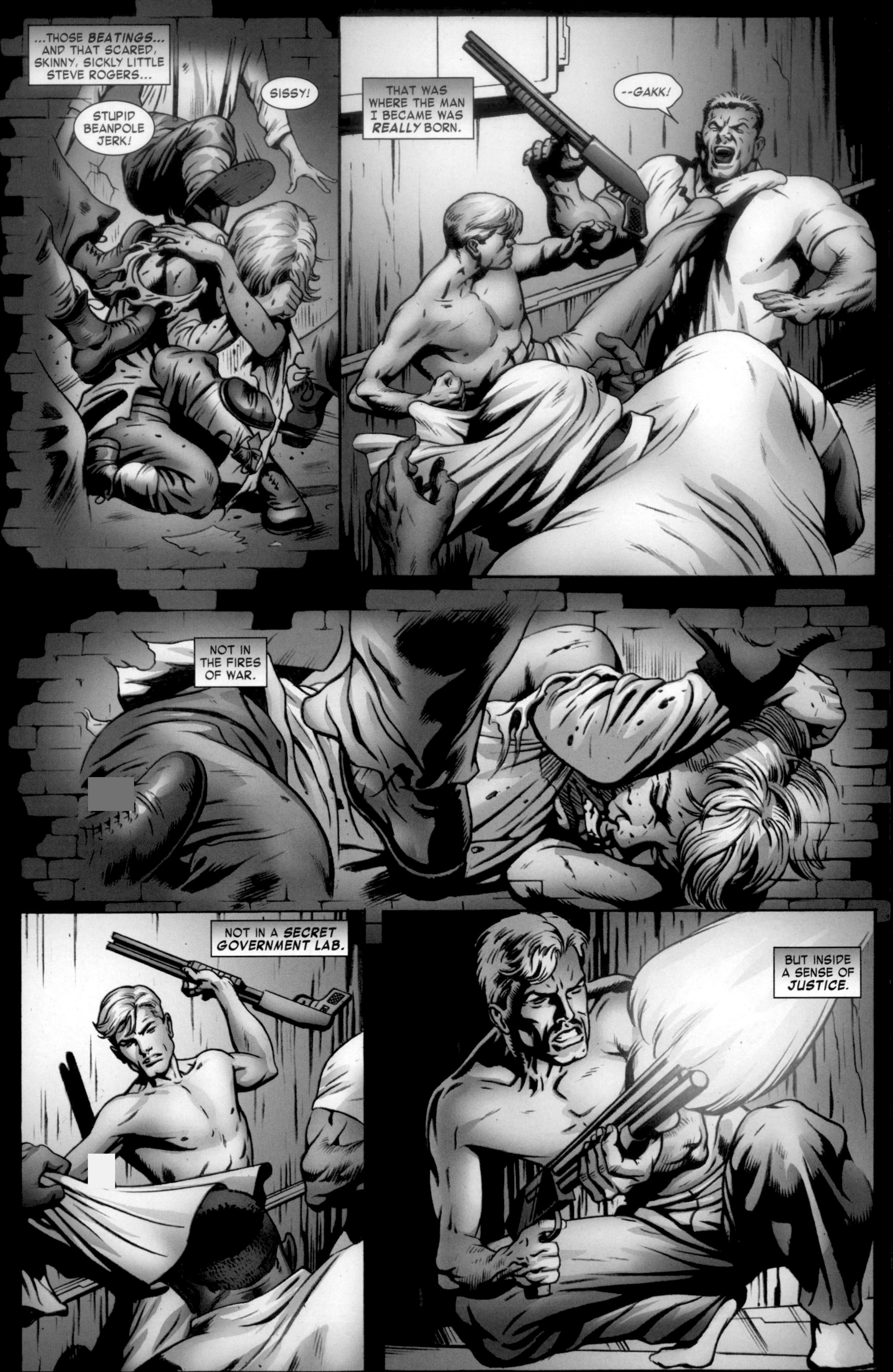
...THOSE BEATINGS... AND THAT SCARED, SKINNY, SICKLY LITTLE STEVE ROGERS...
SISSY!
STUPID BEANPOLE JERK!
THAT WAS WHERE THE MAN I BECAME WAS REALLY BORN.
--GAKK!
NOT IN THE FIRES OF WAR.
NOT IN A SECRET GOVERNMENT LAB.
BUT INSIDE A SENSE OF JUSTICE.

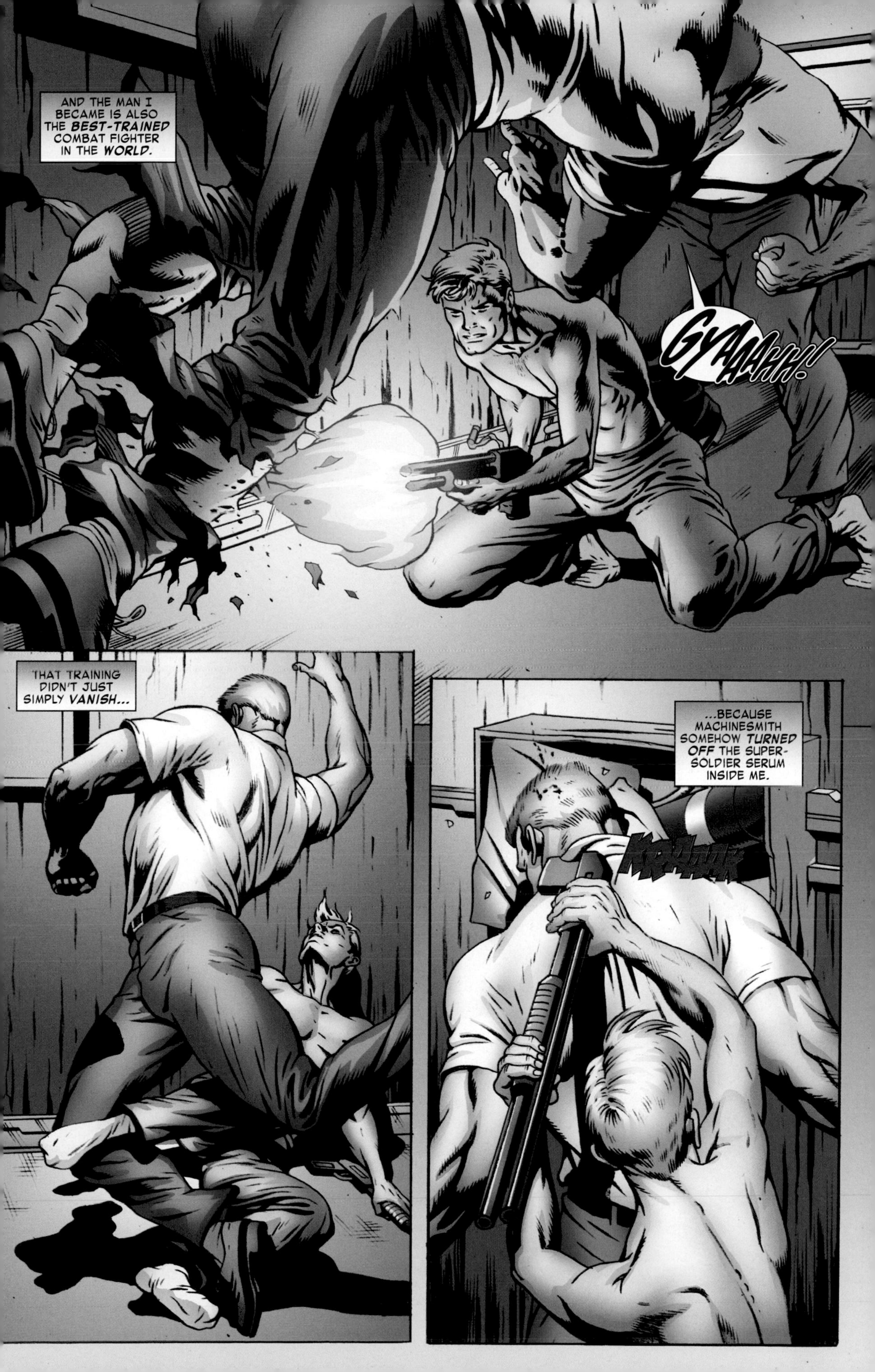
AND THE MAN I BECAME IS ALSO THE BEST-TRAINED COMBAT FIGHTER IN THE WORLD.
GYAAAHH!
THAT TRAINING DIDN'T JUST SIMPLY VANISH...
...BECAUSE MACHINESMITH SOMEHOW TURNED OFF THE SUPER-SOLDIER SERUM INSIDE ME.

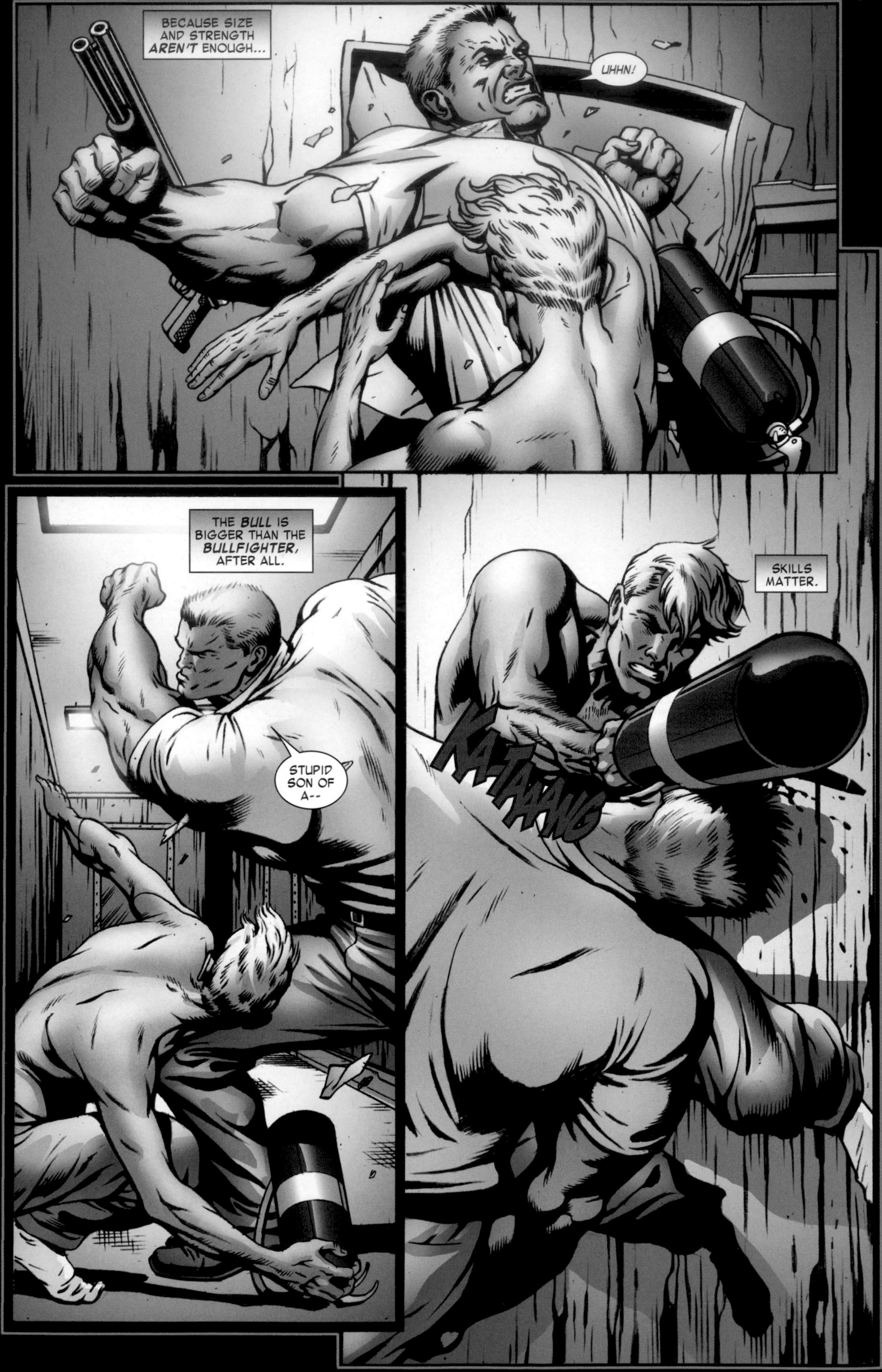
BECAUSE SIZE AND STRENGTH AREN'T ENOUGH...
UHHN!
THE BULL IS BIGGER THAN THE BULLFIGHTER, AFTER ALL.
STUPID SON OF A--
SKILLS MATTER.
KA-TAAANG

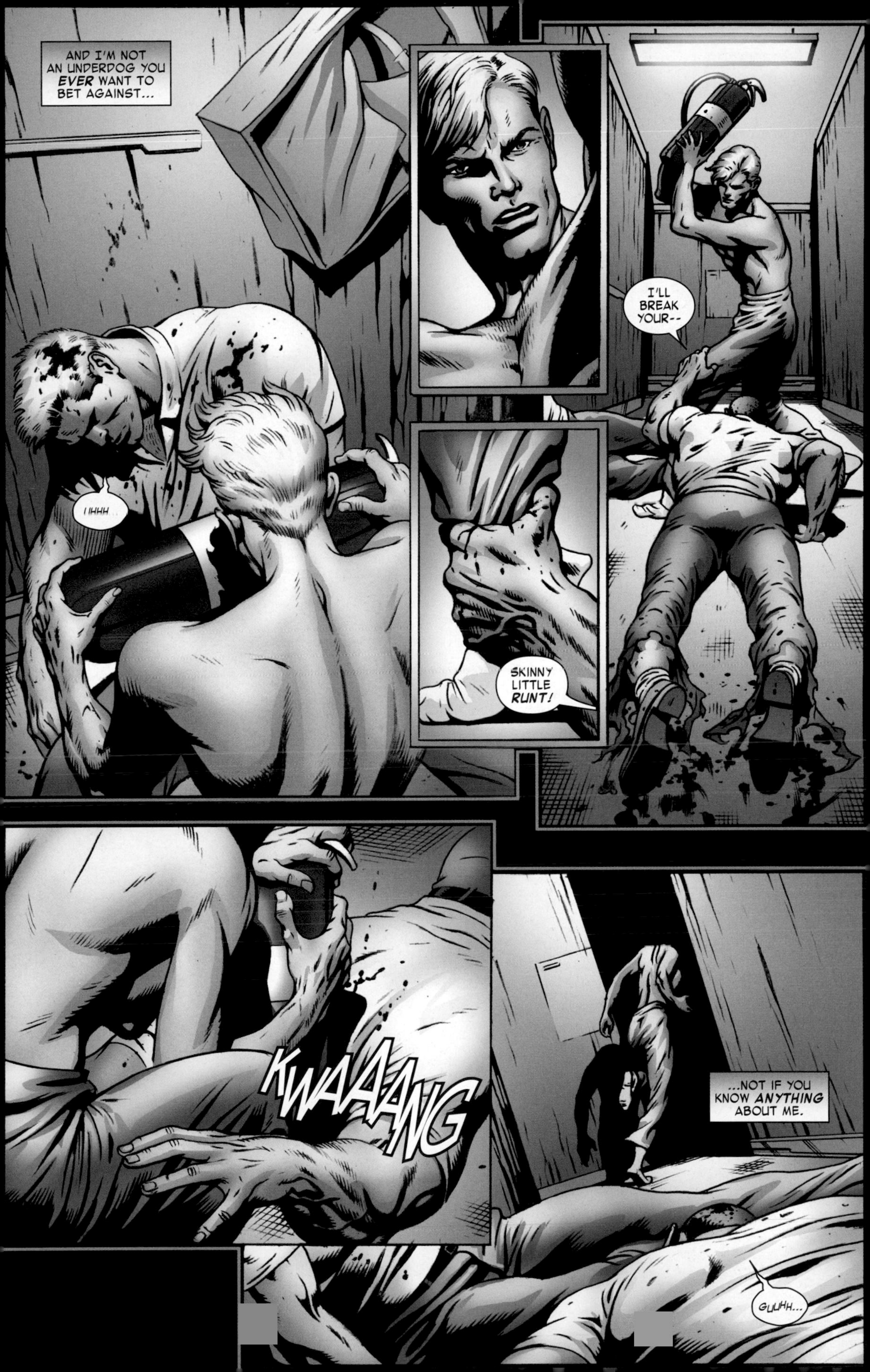
AND I'M NOT AN UNDERDOG YOU EVER WANT TO BET AGAINST...
UHHH...
SKINNY LITTLE RUNT!
I'LL BREAK YOUR--
KWAAAANG
...NOT IF YOU KNOW ANYTHING ABOUT ME.
GUUHH...

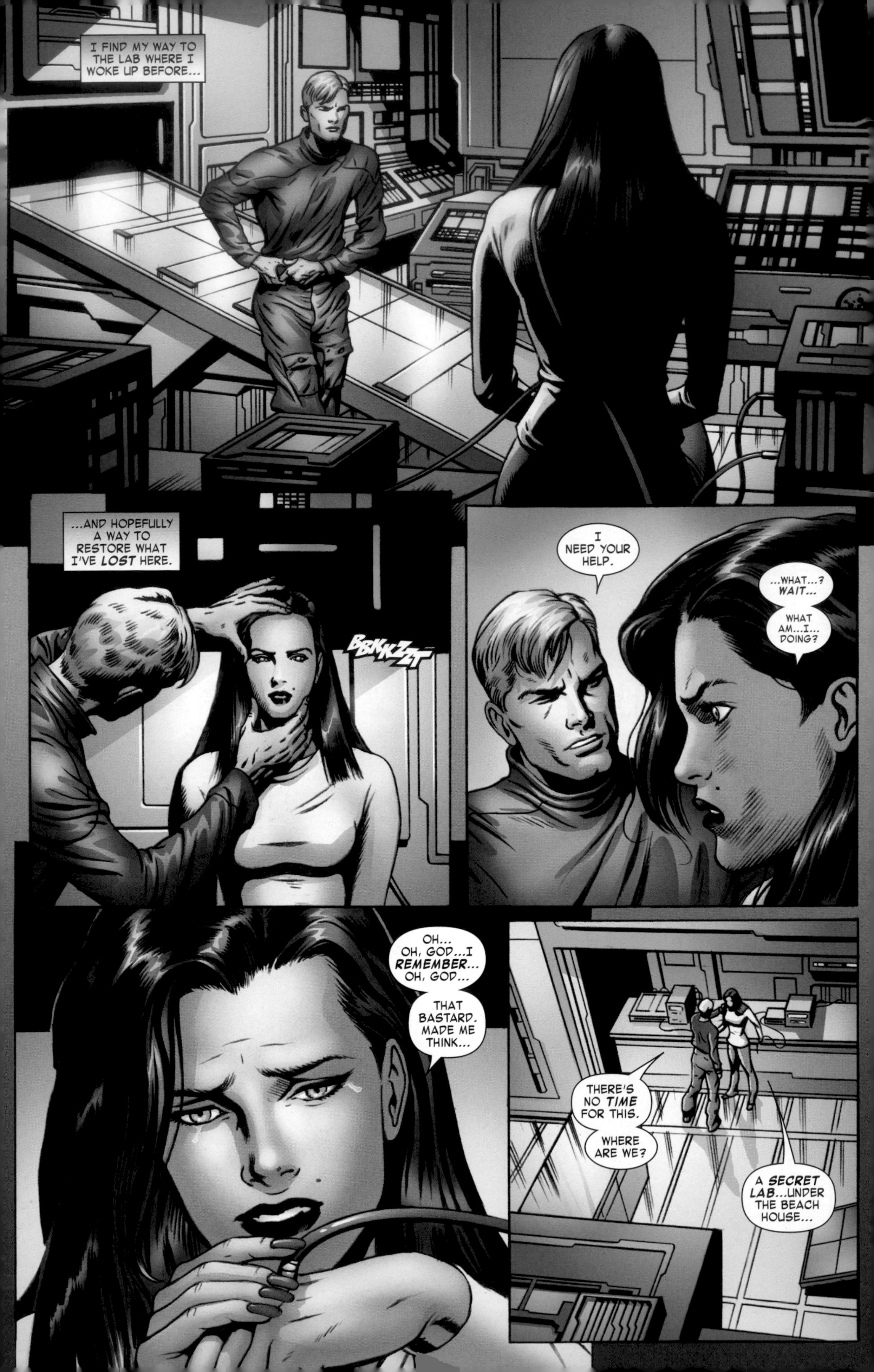
I FIND MY WAY TO THE LAB WHERE I WOKE UP BEFORE...
...AND HOPEFULLY A WAY TO RESTORE WHAT I'VE LOST HERE.
BBKKZZT
I NEED YOUR HELP.
...WHAT...? WAIT...
WHAT AM...I... DOING?
OH... OH, GOD...I REMEMBER... OH, GOD...
THAT BASTARD. MADE ME THINK...
THERE'S NO TIME FOR THIS.
WHERE ARE WE?
A SECRET LAB...UNDER THE BEACH HOUSE...

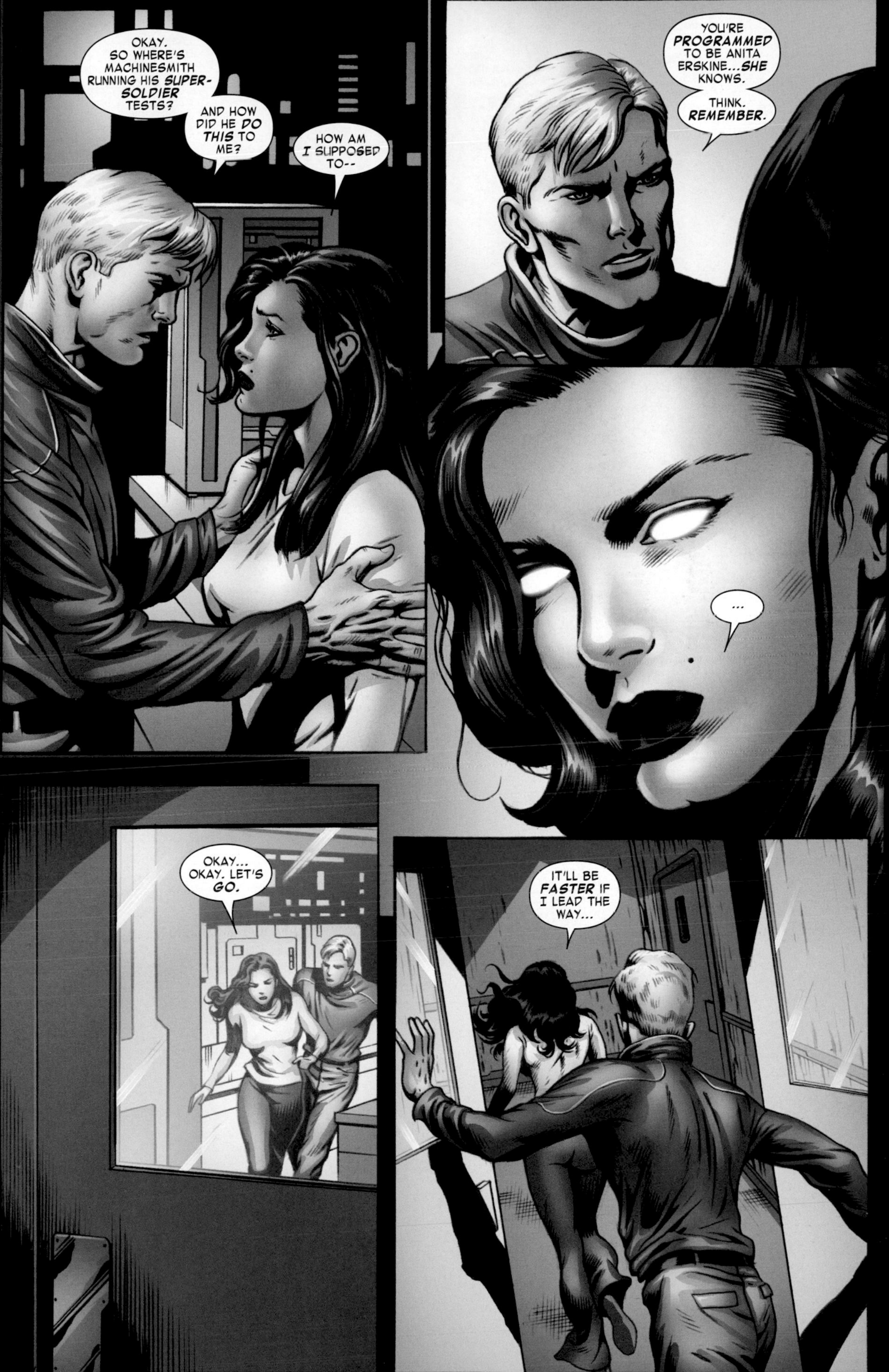
OKAY. SO WHERE'S MACHINESMITH RUNNING HIS SUPER-SOLDIER TESTS?
AND HOW DID HE DO THIS TO ME?
HOW AM I SUPPOSED TO--
YOU'RE PROGRAMMED TO BE ANITA ERSKINE...SHE KNOWS.
THINK. REMEMBER.
...
OKAY... OKAY. LET'S GO.
IT'LL BE FASTER IF I LEAD THE WAY...

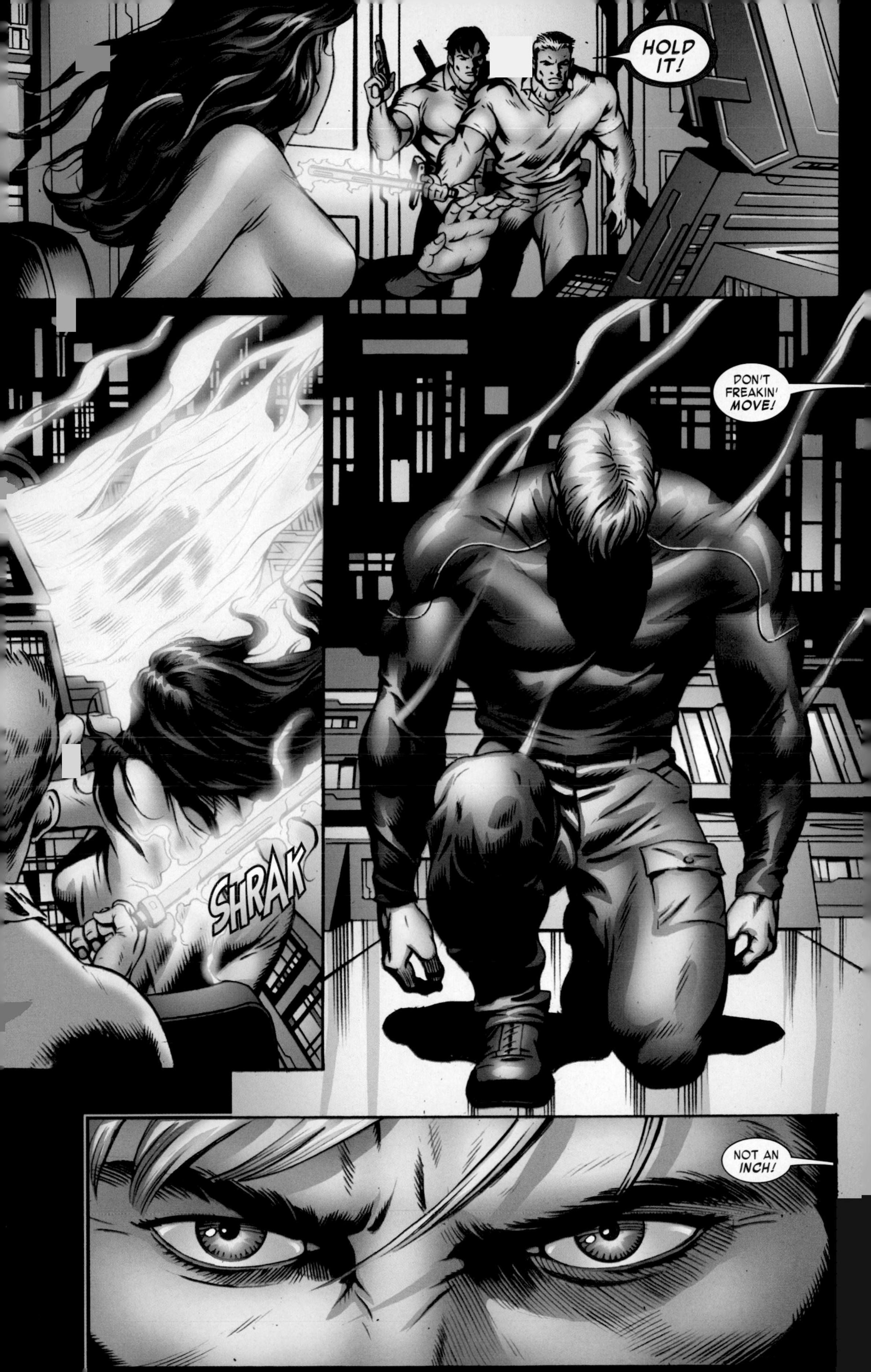
HOLD IT!
DON'T FREAKIN' MOVE!
SHRAK
NOT AN INCH!

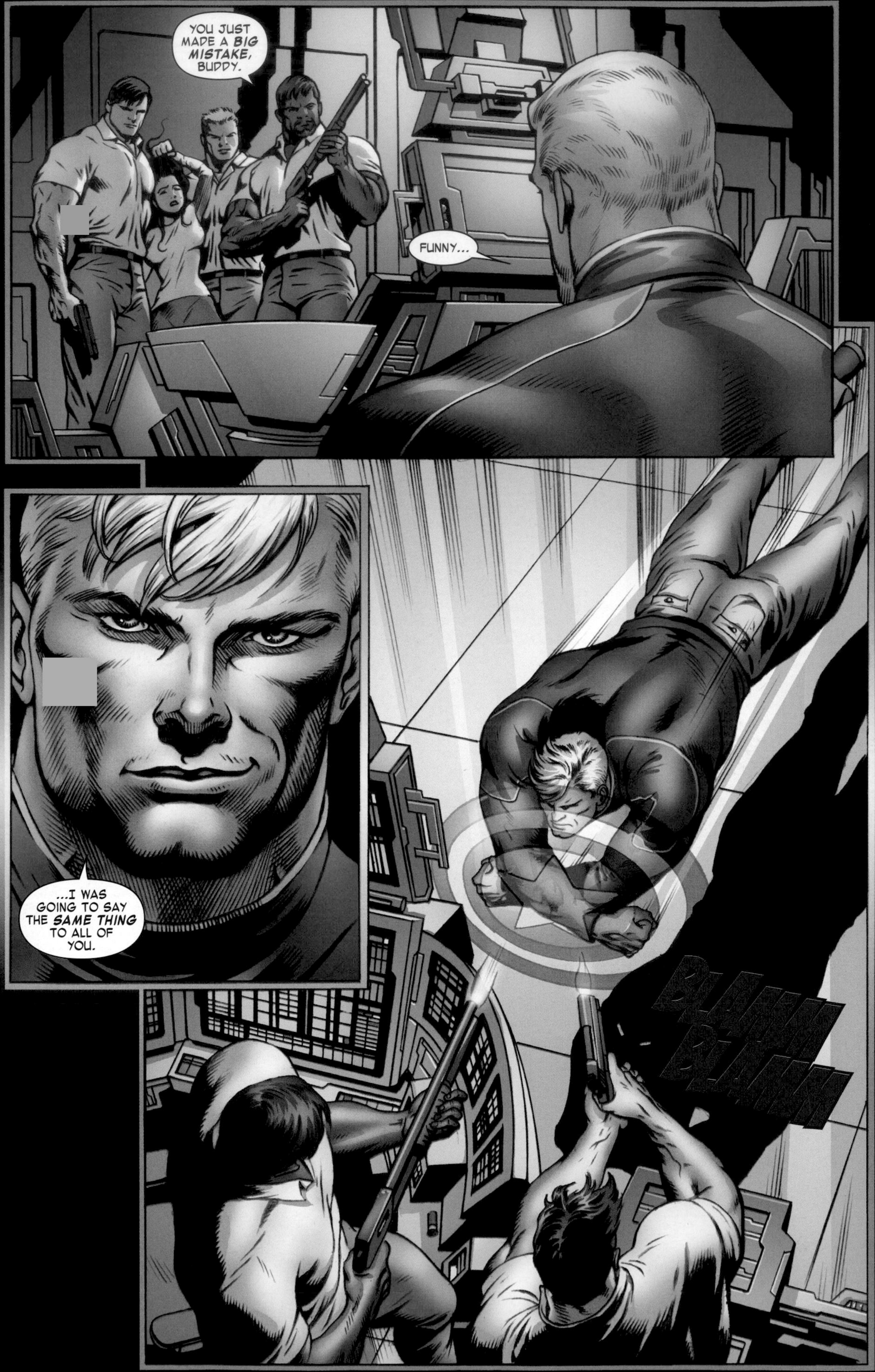
YOU JUST MADE A BIG MISTAKE, BUDDY.
FUNNY...
...I WAS GOING TO SAY THE SAME THING TO ALL OF YOU.

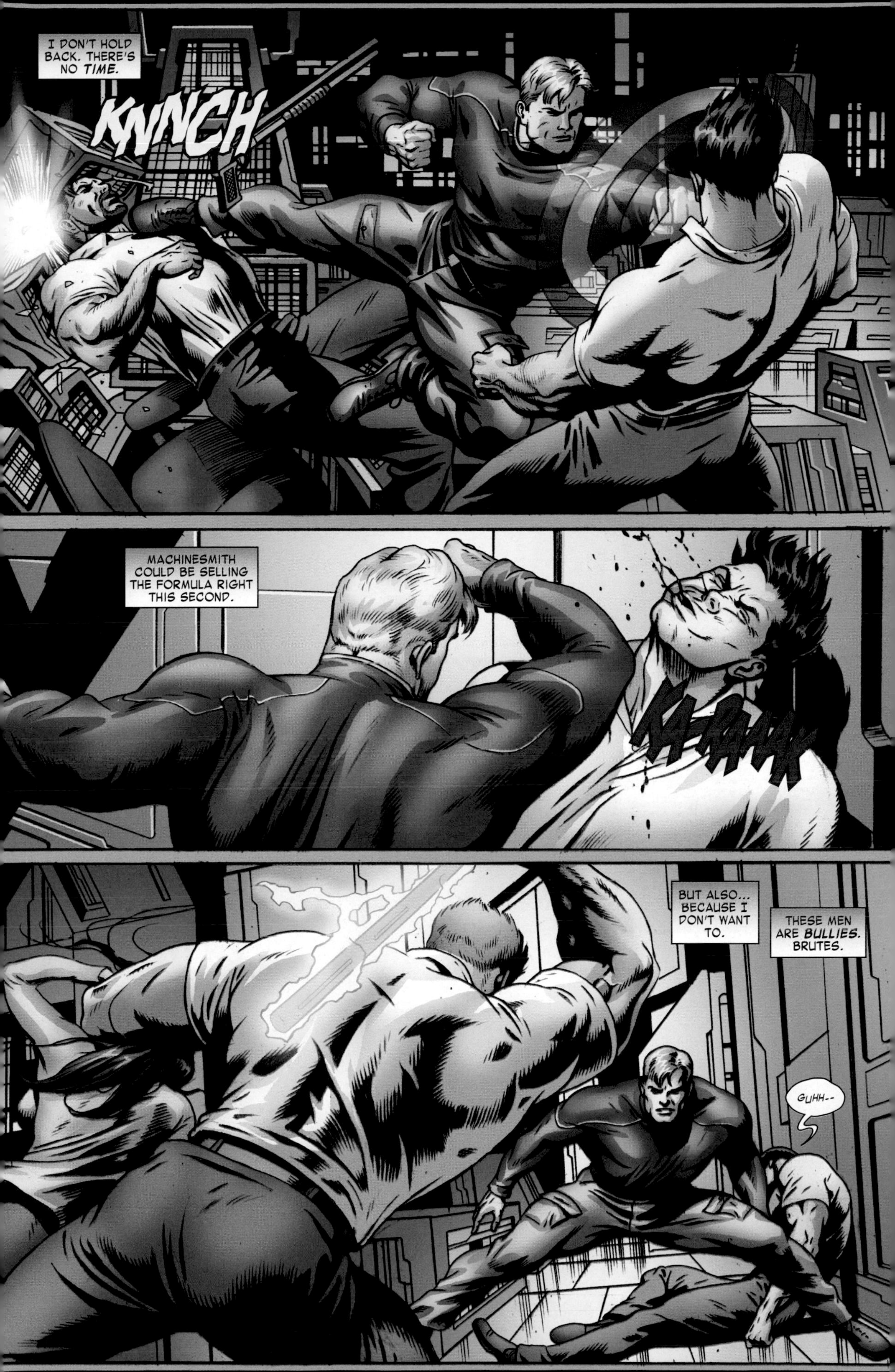
I DON'T HOLD BACK. THERE'S NO *TIME.*
KNNCH
MACHINESMITH COULD BE SELLING THE FORMULA RIGHT THIS SECOND.
KA-RAAAK
BUT ALSO... BECAUSE I DON'T WANT TO.
THESE MEN ARE *BULLIES.* BRUTES.
GUHH--

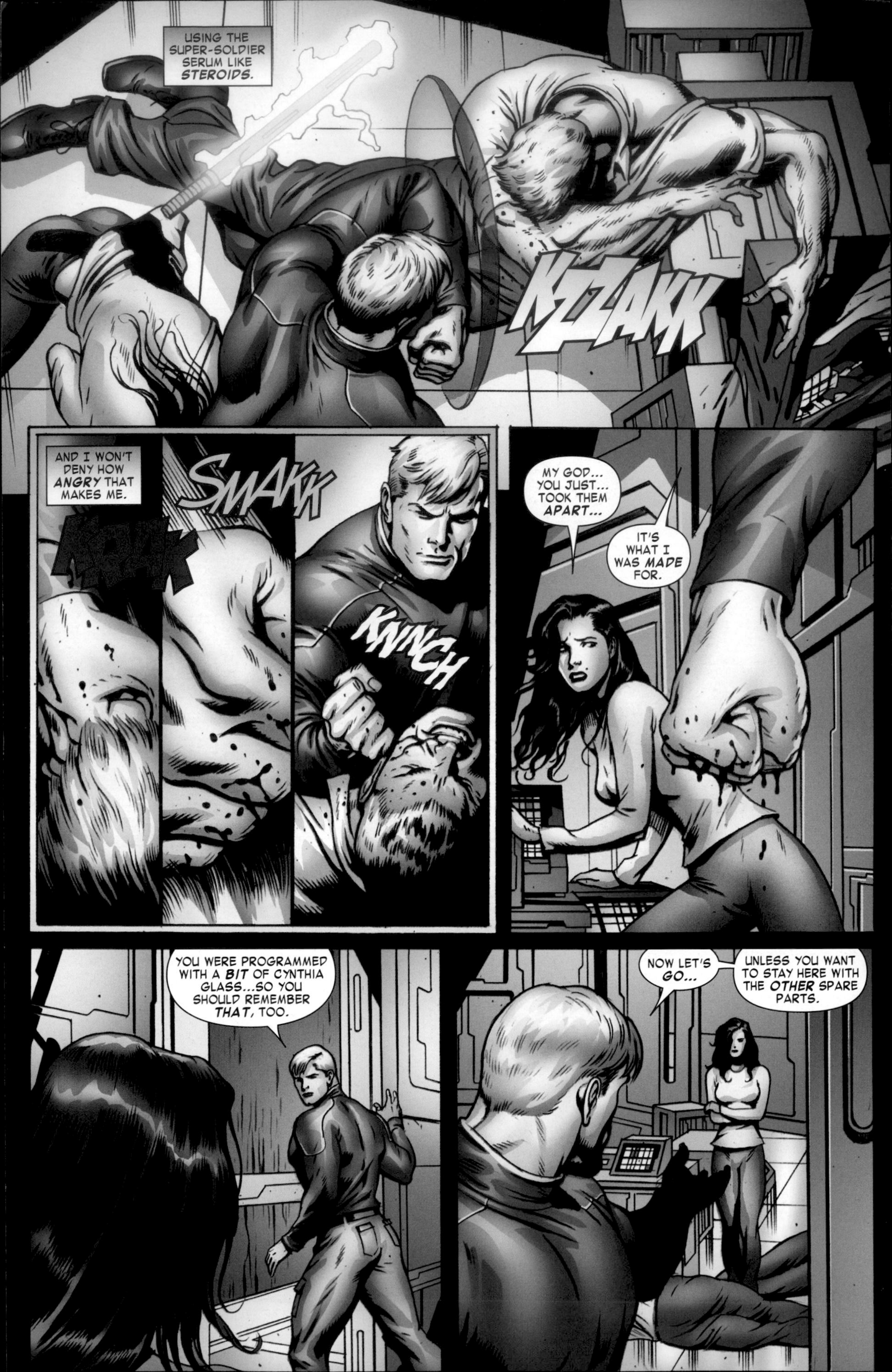
USING THE SUPER-SOLDIER SERUM LIKE STEROIDS.
KZZAKK
AND I WON'T DENY HOW ANGRY THAT MAKES ME.
SMAKK
KNNCH
MY GOD... YOU JUST... TOOK THEM APART...
IT'S WHAT I WAS MADE FOR.
YOU WERE PROGRAMMED WITH A BIT OF CYNTHIA GLASS...SO YOU SHOULD REMEMBER THAT, TOO.
NOW LET'S GO...
UNLESS YOU WANT TO STAY HERE WITH THE OTHER SPARE PARTS.

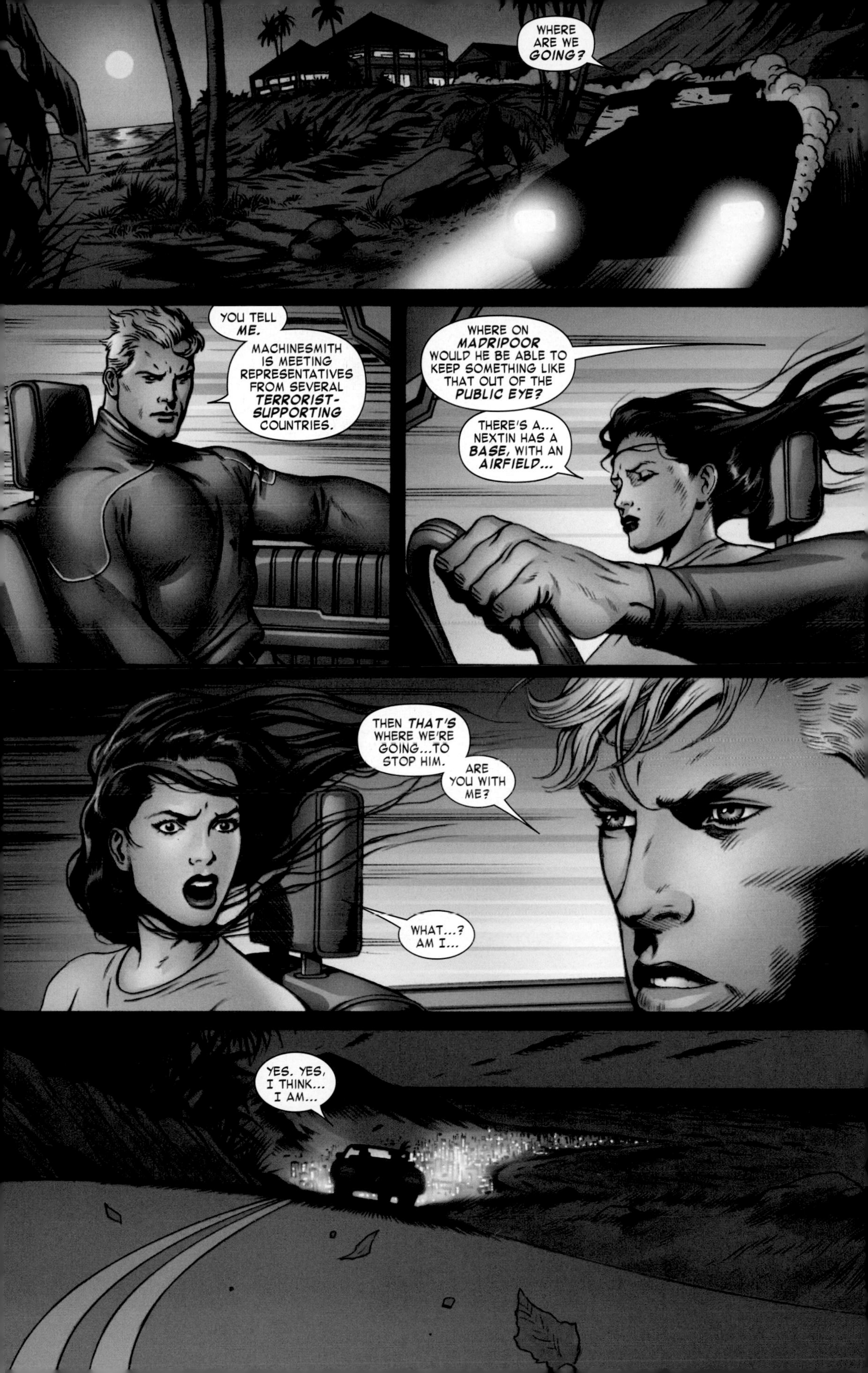
WHERE ARE WE GOING?
YOU TELL ME.
MACHINESMITH IS MEETING REPRESENTATIVES FROM SEVERAL TERRORIST-SUPPORTING COUNTRIES.
WHERE ON MADRIPOOR WOULD HE BE ABLE TO KEEP SOMETHING LIKE THAT OUT OF THE PUBLIC EYE?
THERE'S A... NEXTIN HAS A BASE, WITH AN AIRFIELD...
THEN THAT'S WHERE WE'RE GOING...TO STOP HIM.
ARE YOU WITH ME?
WHAT...? AM I...
YES. YES, I THINK... I AM...

4

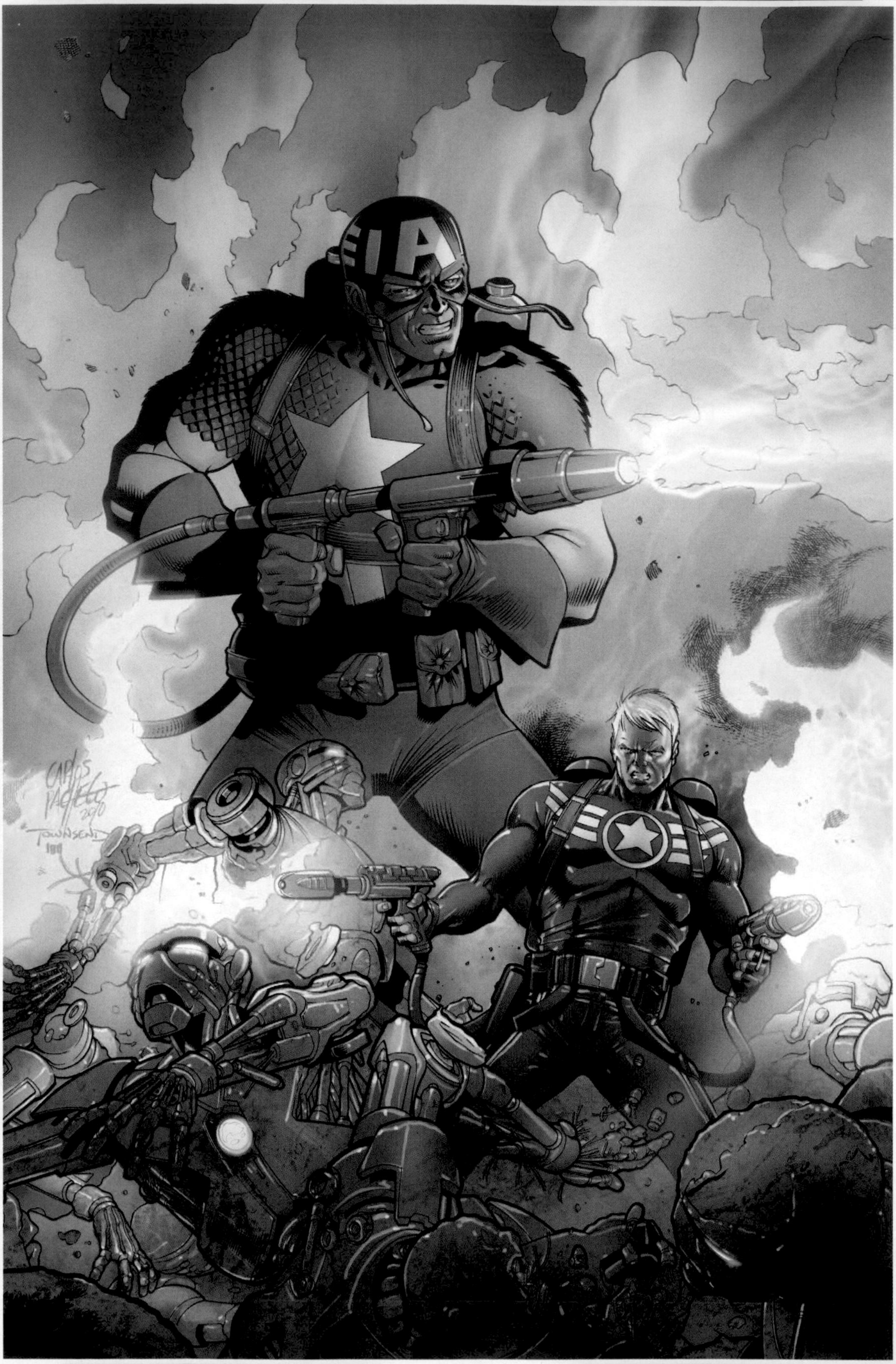
CARLOS PACHECO 2010
TOWNSEND

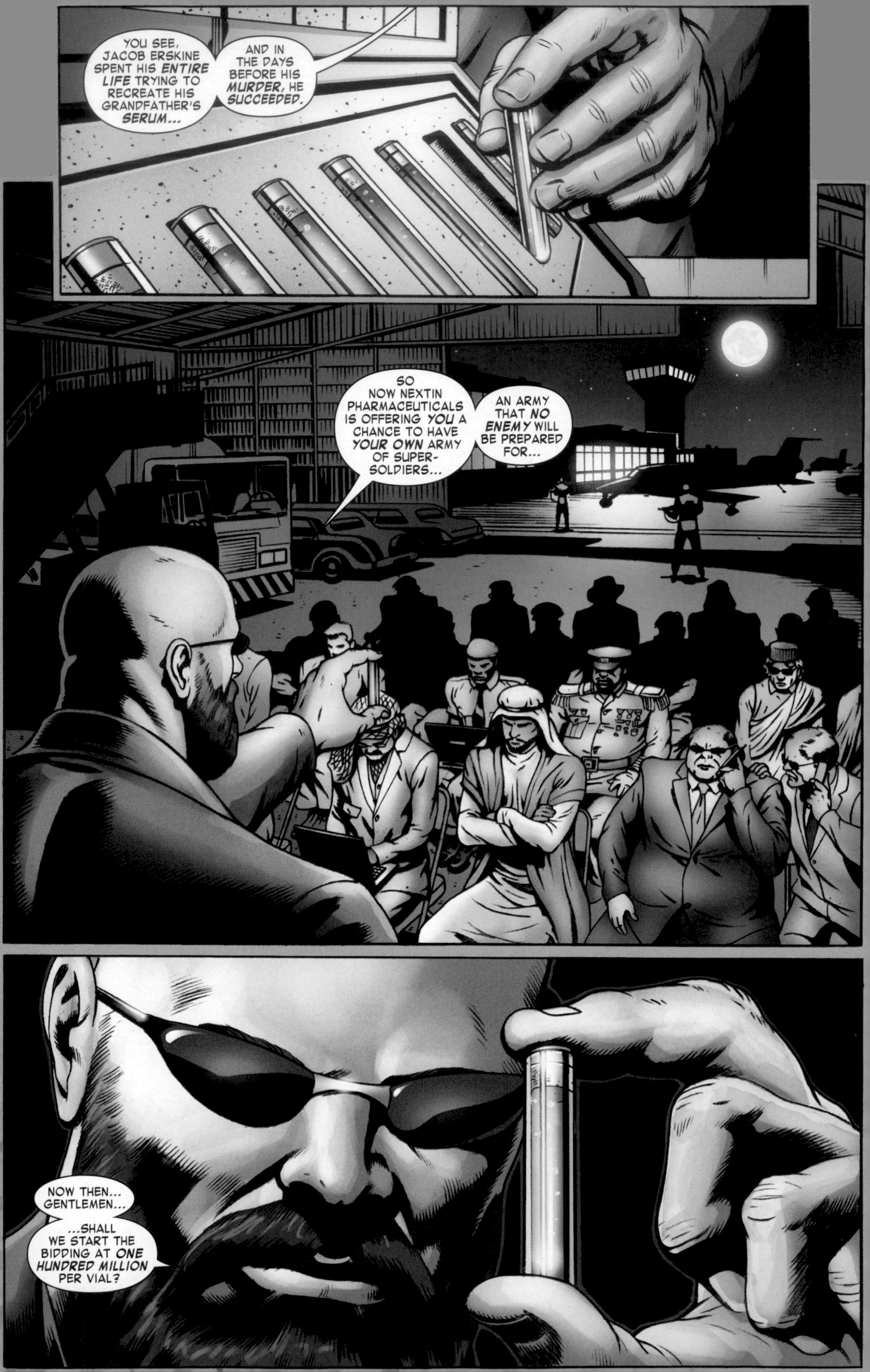
YOU SEE, JACOB ERSKINE SPENT HIS ENTIRE LIFE TRYING TO RECREATE HIS GRANDFATHER'S SERUM...
AND IN THE DAYS BEFORE HIS MURDER, HE SUCCEEDED.
SO NOW NEXTIN PHARMACEUTICALS IS OFFERING YOU A CHANCE TO HAVE YOUR OWN ARMY OF SUPER-SOLDIERS...
AN ARMY THAT NO ENEMY WILL BE PREPARED FOR...
NOW THEN... GENTLEMEN...
...SHALL WE START THE BIDDING AT ONE HUNDRED MILLION PER VIAL?

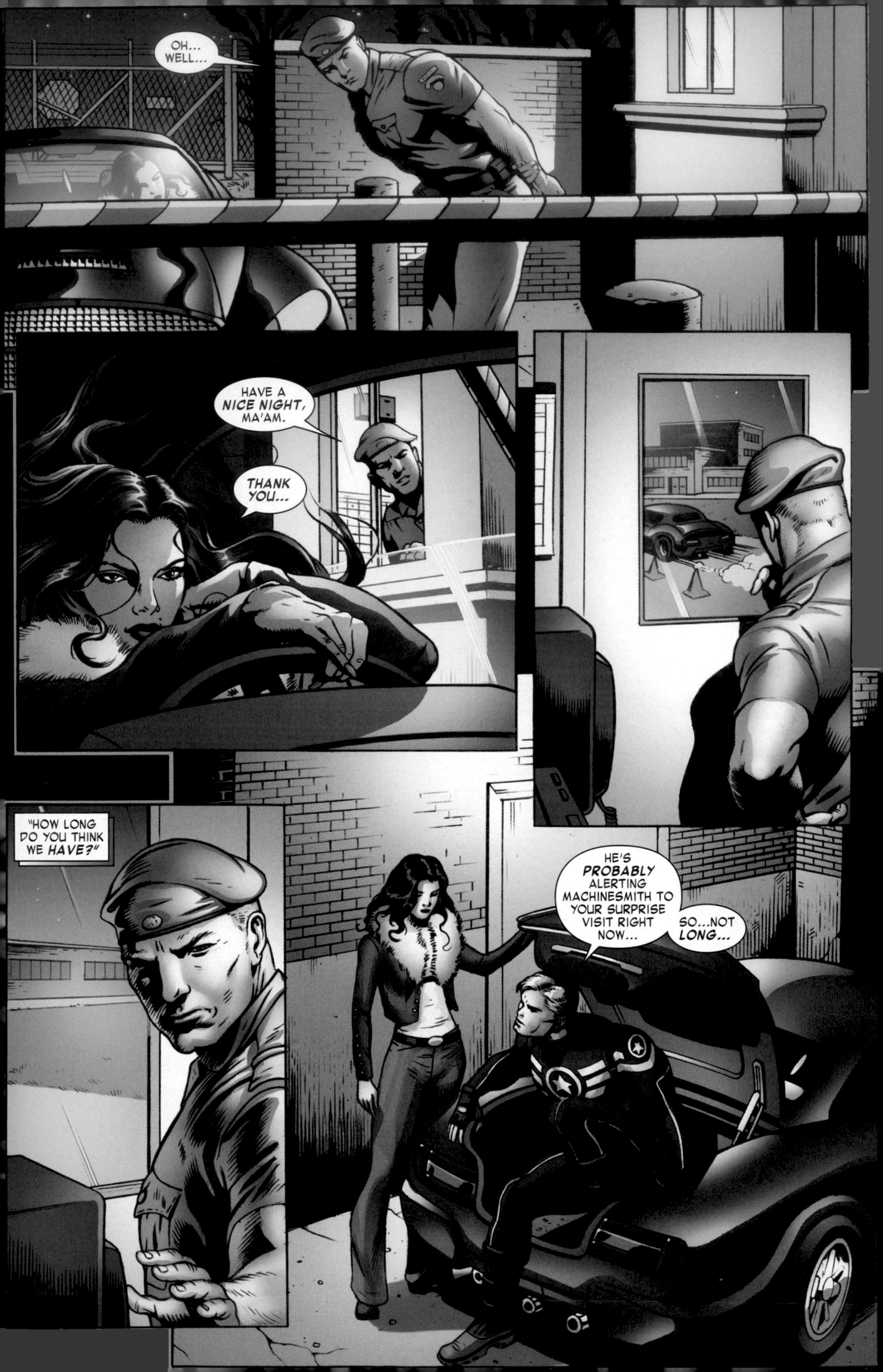
OH... WELL...
HAVE A NICE NIGHT, MA'AM.
THANK YOU...
"HOW LONG DO YOU THINK WE HAVE?"
HE'S PROBABLY ALERTING MACHINESMITH TO YOUR SURPRISE VISIT RIGHT NOW...
SO...NOT LONG...

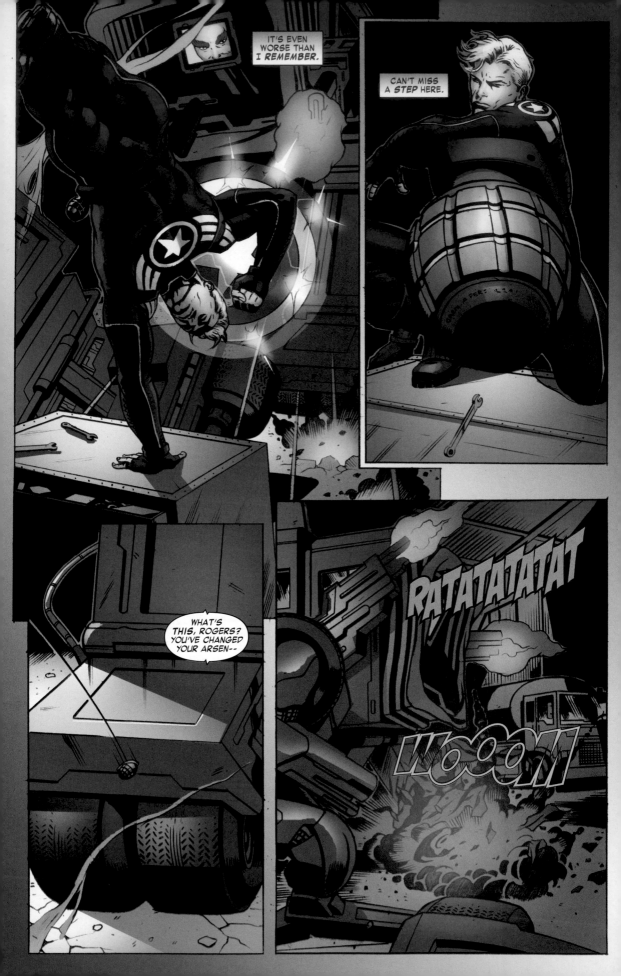

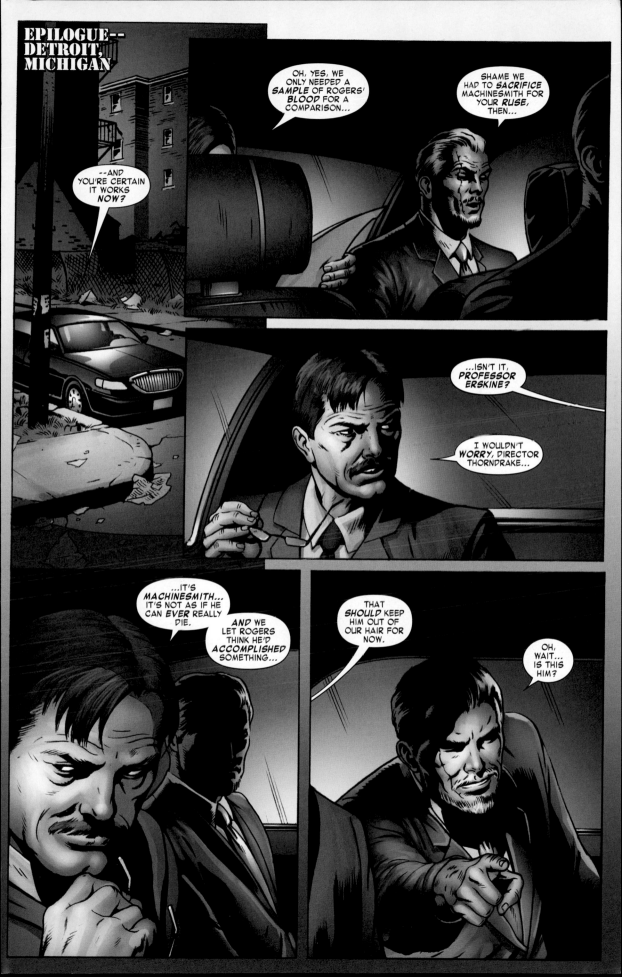

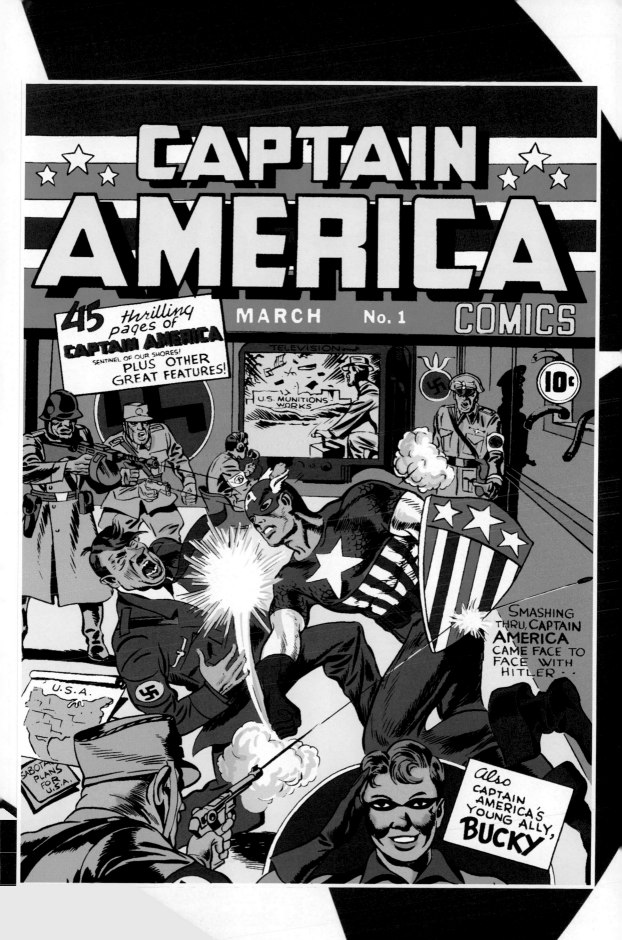

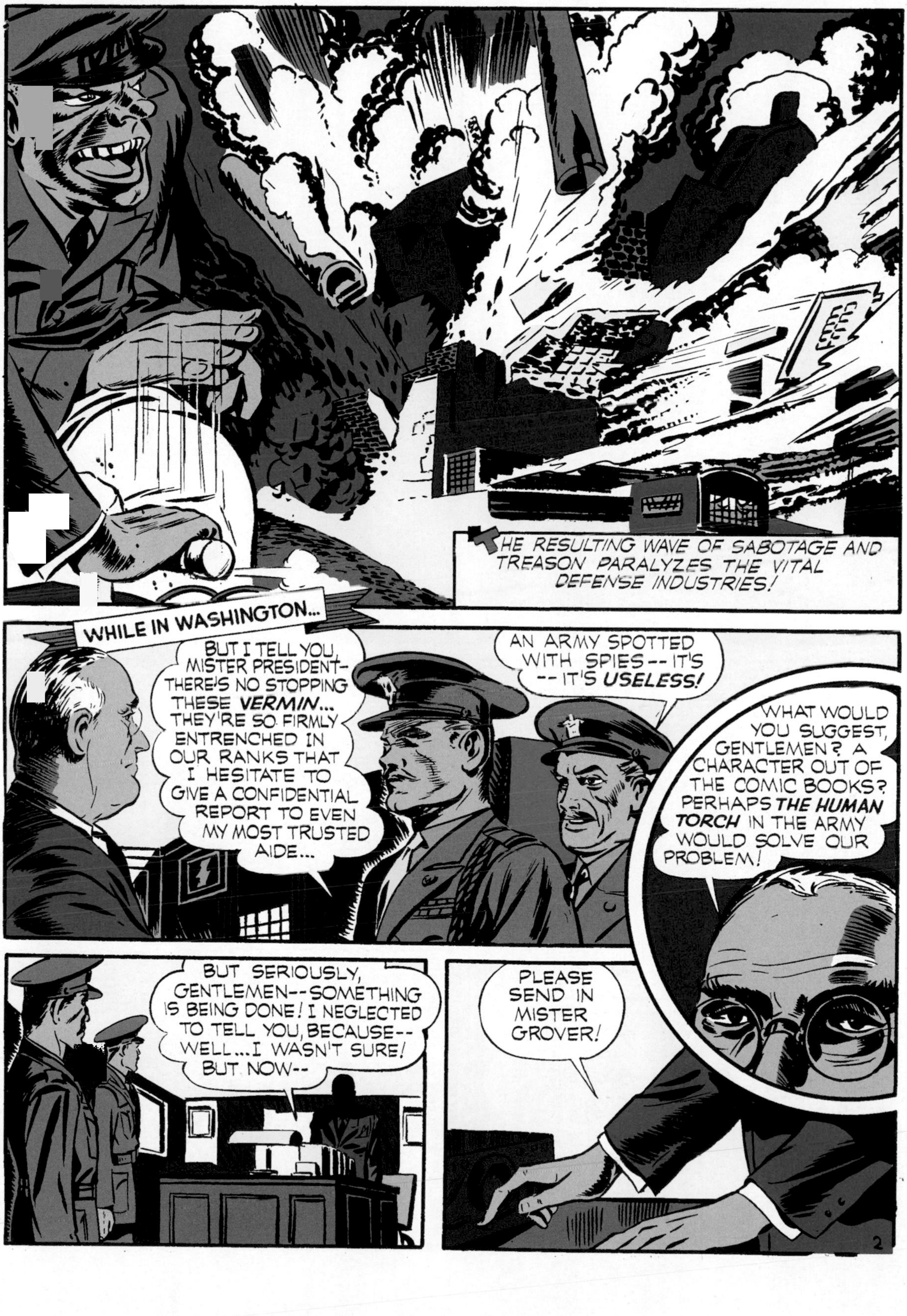
THE RESULTING WAVE OF SABOTAGE AND TREASON PARALYZES THE VITAL DEFENSE INDUSTRIES!
WHILE IN WASHINGTON...
BUT I TELL YOU, MISTER PRESIDENT-- THERE'S NO STOPPING THESE VERMIN... THEY'RE SO FIRMLY ENTRENCHED IN OUR RANKS THAT I HESITATE TO GIVE A CONFIDENTIAL REPORT TO EVEN MY MOST TRUSTED AIDE...
AN ARMY SPOTTED WITH SPIES -- IT'S -- IT'S USELESS!
WHAT WOULD YOU SUGGEST, GENTLEMEN? A CHARACTER OUT OF THE COMIC BOOKS? PERHAPS THE HUMAN TORCH IN THE ARMY WOULD SOLVE OUR PROBLEM!
BUT SERIOUSLY, GENTLEMEN--SOMETHING IS BEING DONE! I NEGLECTED TO TELL YOU, BECAUSE-- WELL...I WASN'T SURE! BUT NOW--
PLEASE SEND IN MISTER GROVER!
2

#1 VARIANT
BY DAVID FINCH

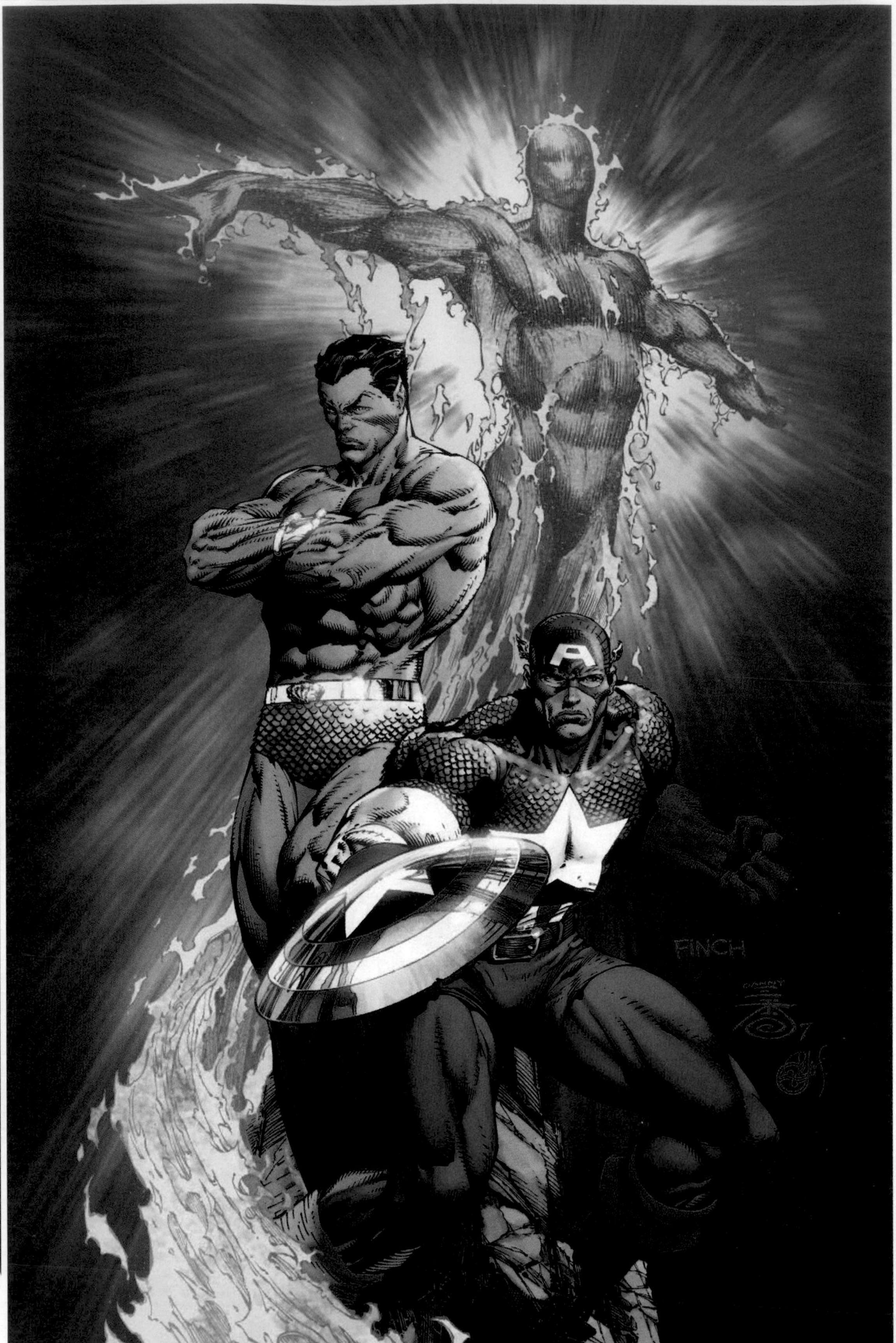
FINCH

#1 SKETCH VARIANT
BY DAVID FINCH

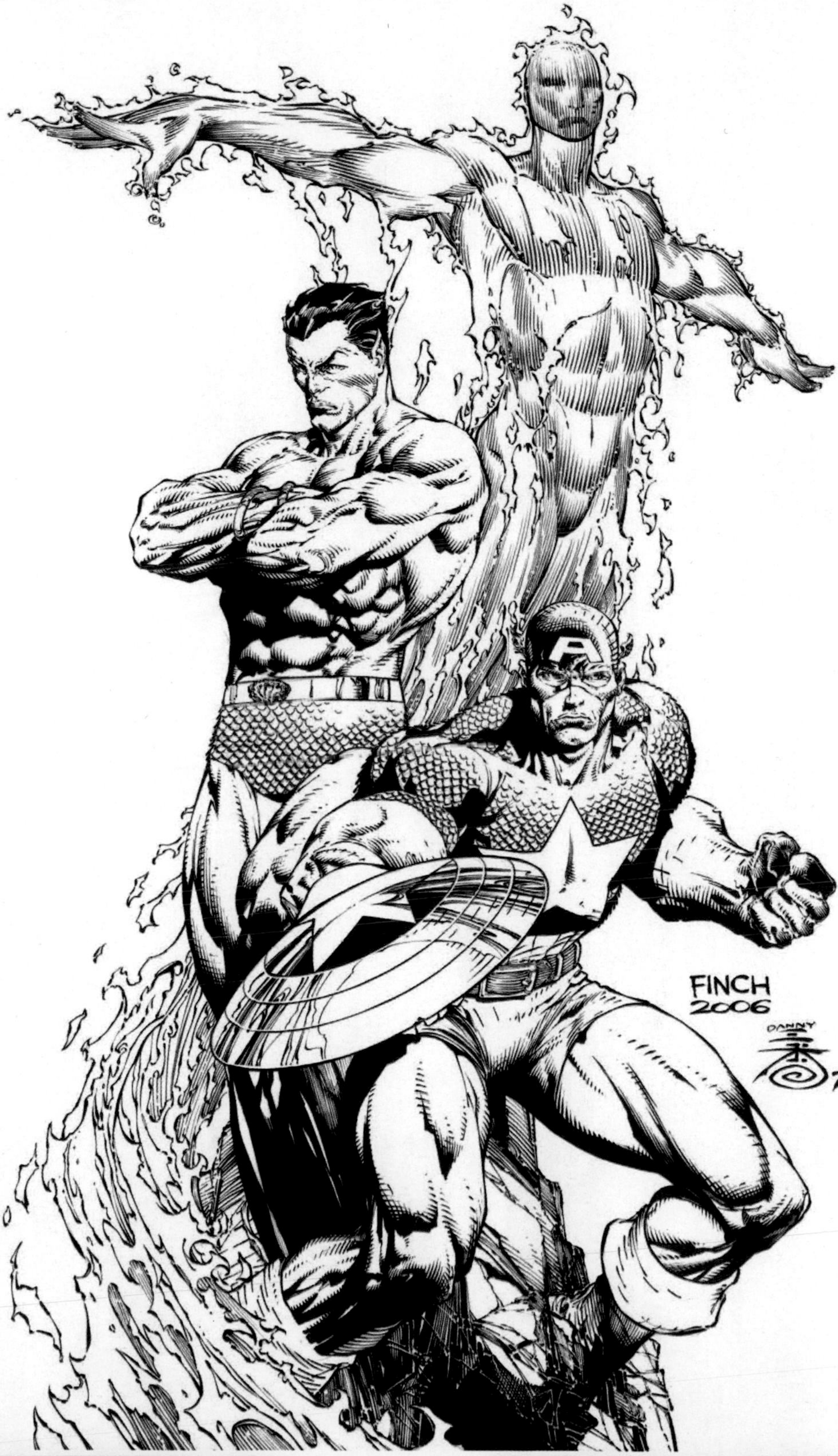
FINCH
2006
DANNY
7

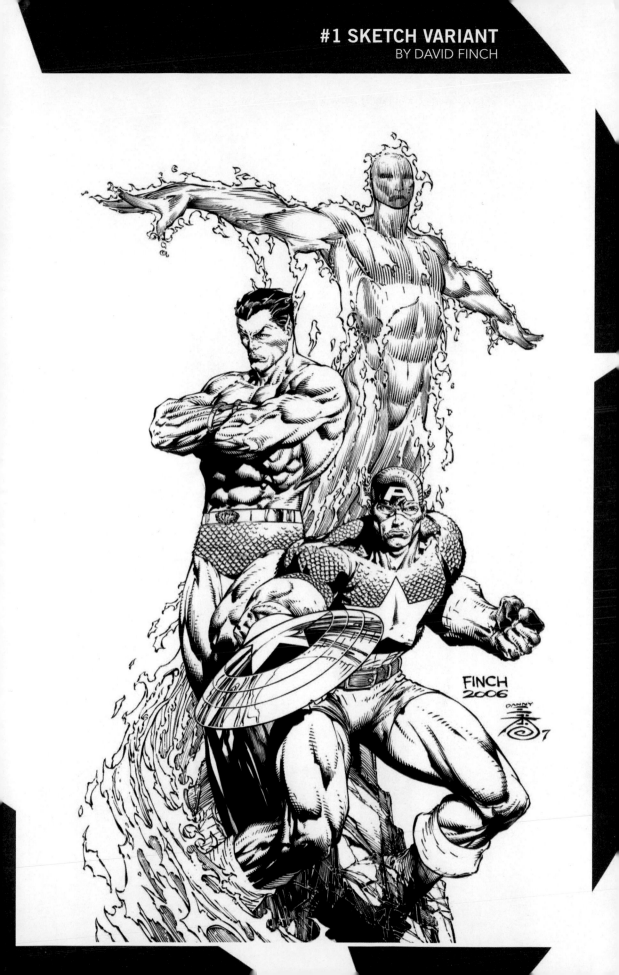

#1 2ND PRINTING VARIANT
BY MARKO DJURDJEVIC

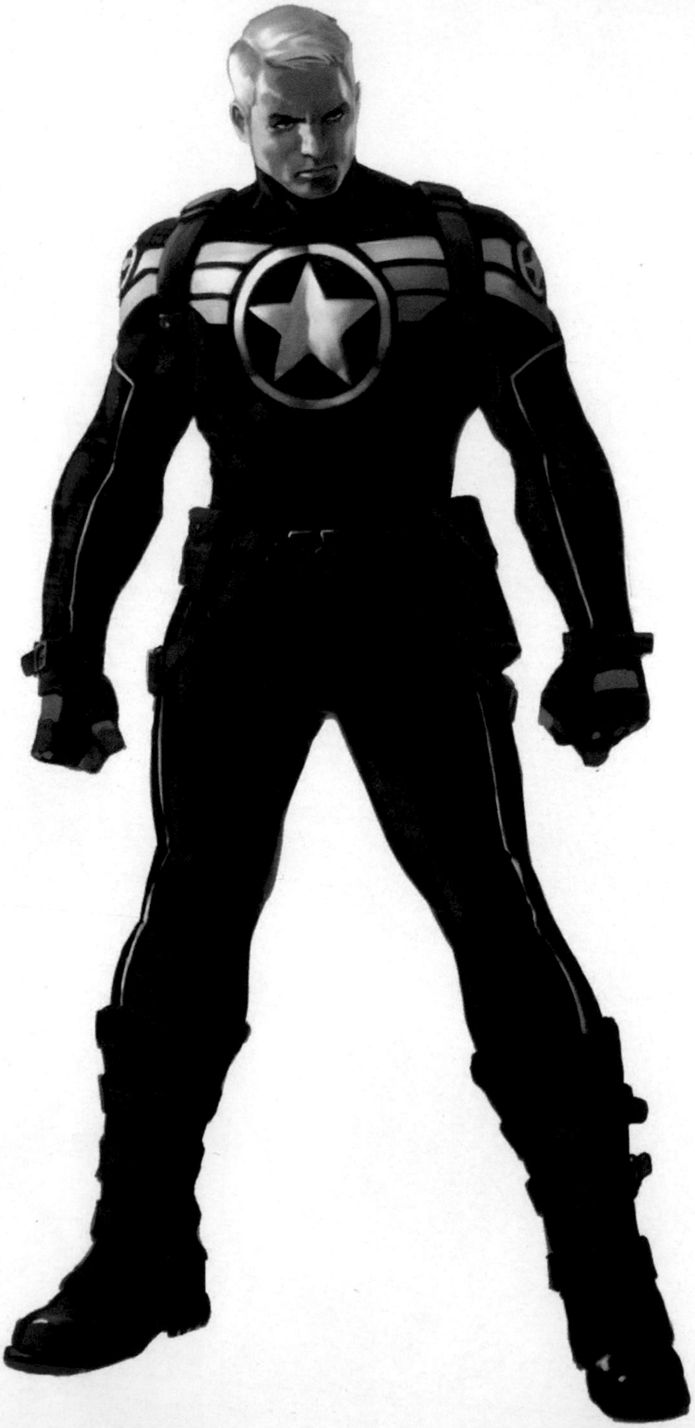

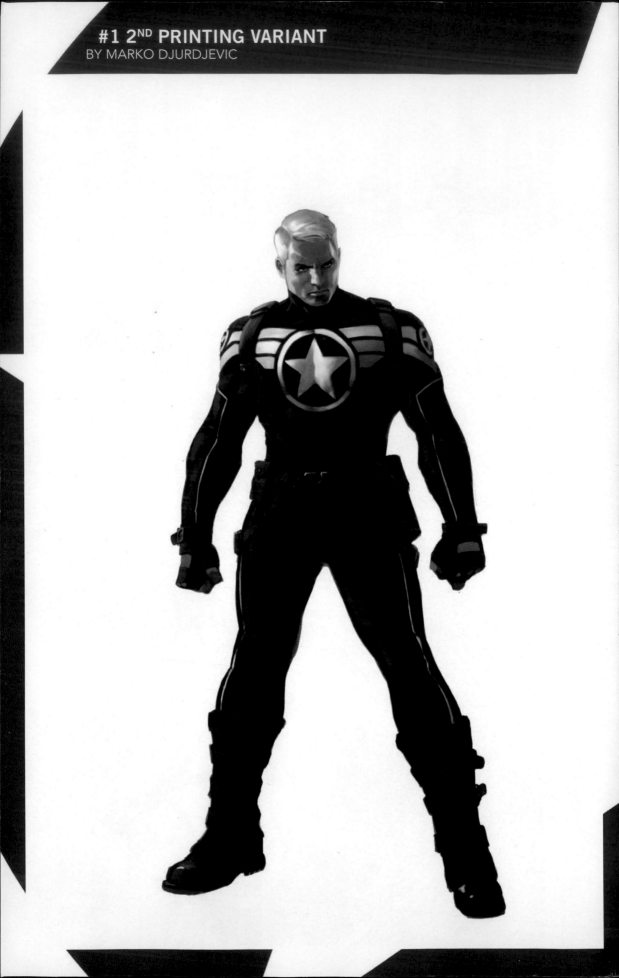

#1 SKETCH VARIANT
BY CARLOS PACHECO

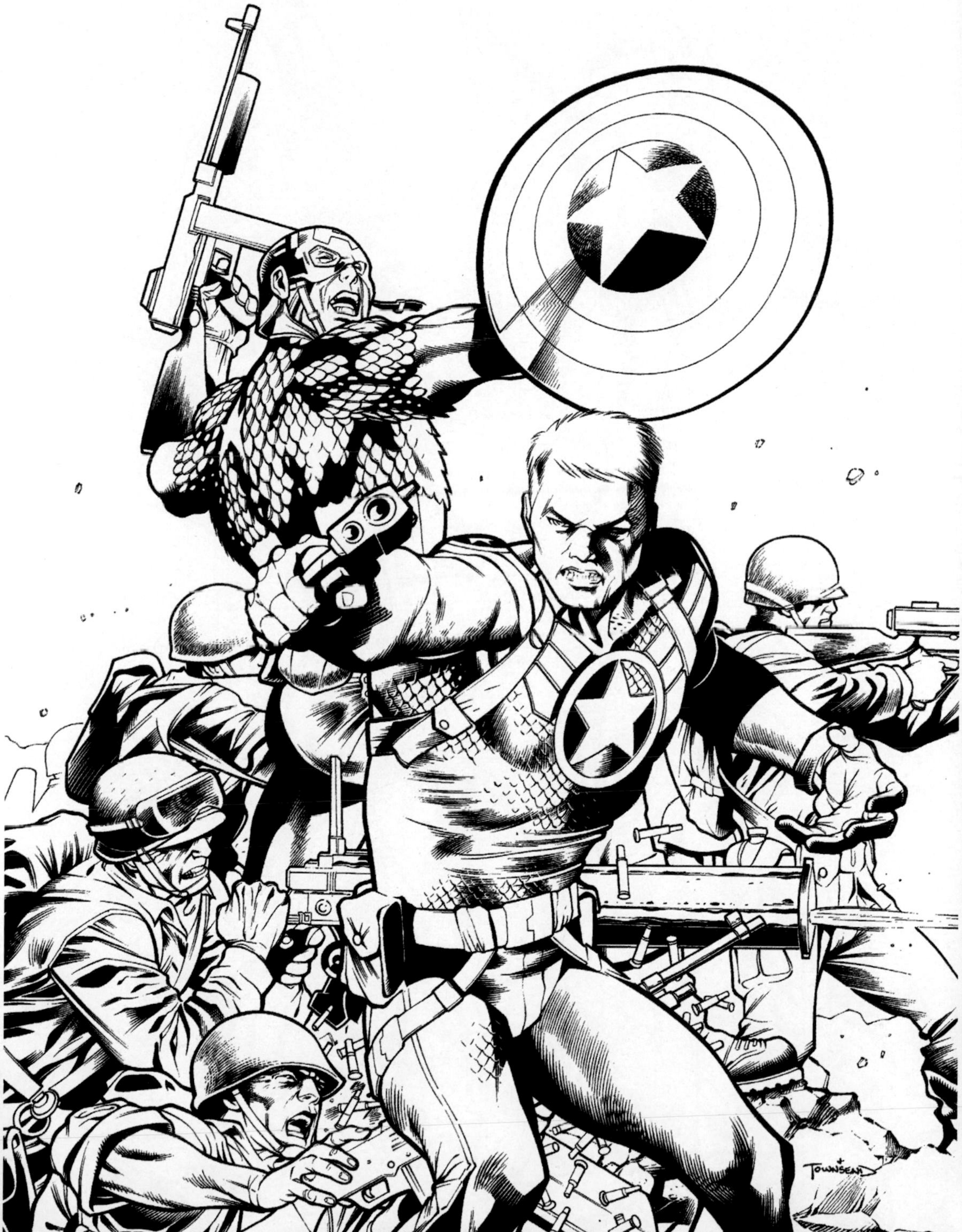
TOWNSEND

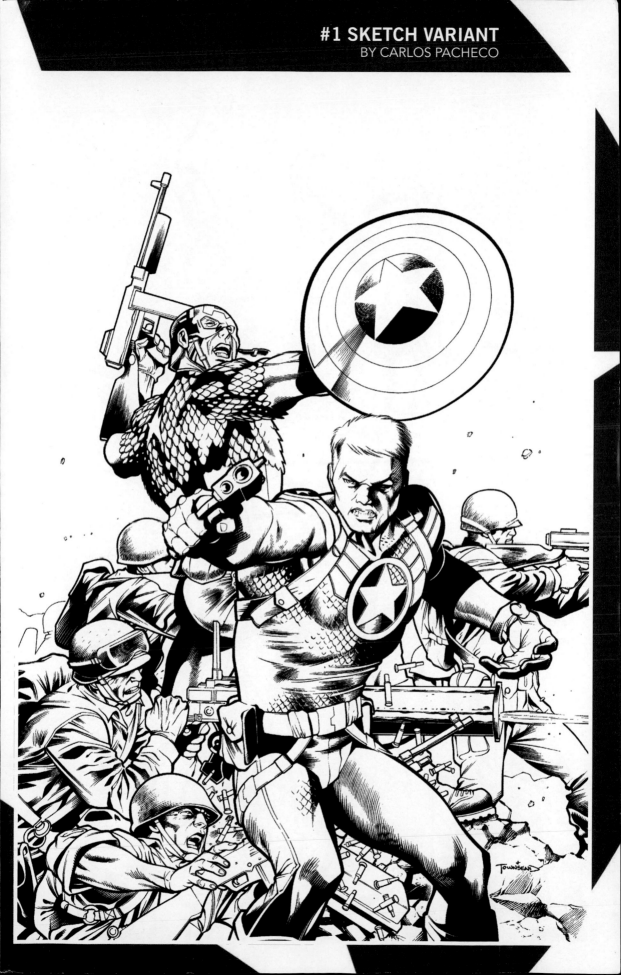

#2 2ND PRINTING VARIANT
BY CARLOS PACHECO

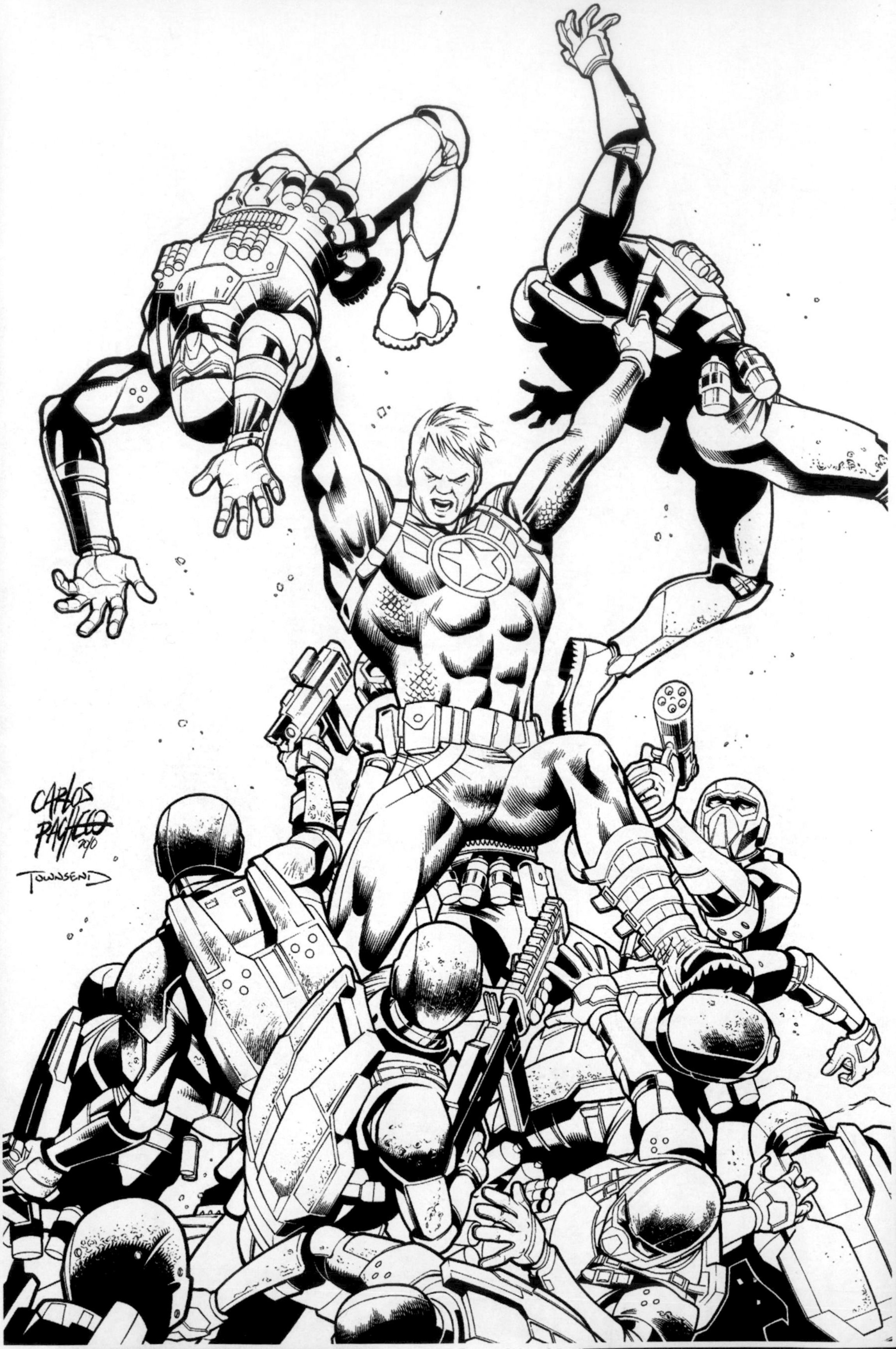

CARLOS PACHECO 2010
TOWNSEND

#3 INKS
BY CARLOS PACHECO

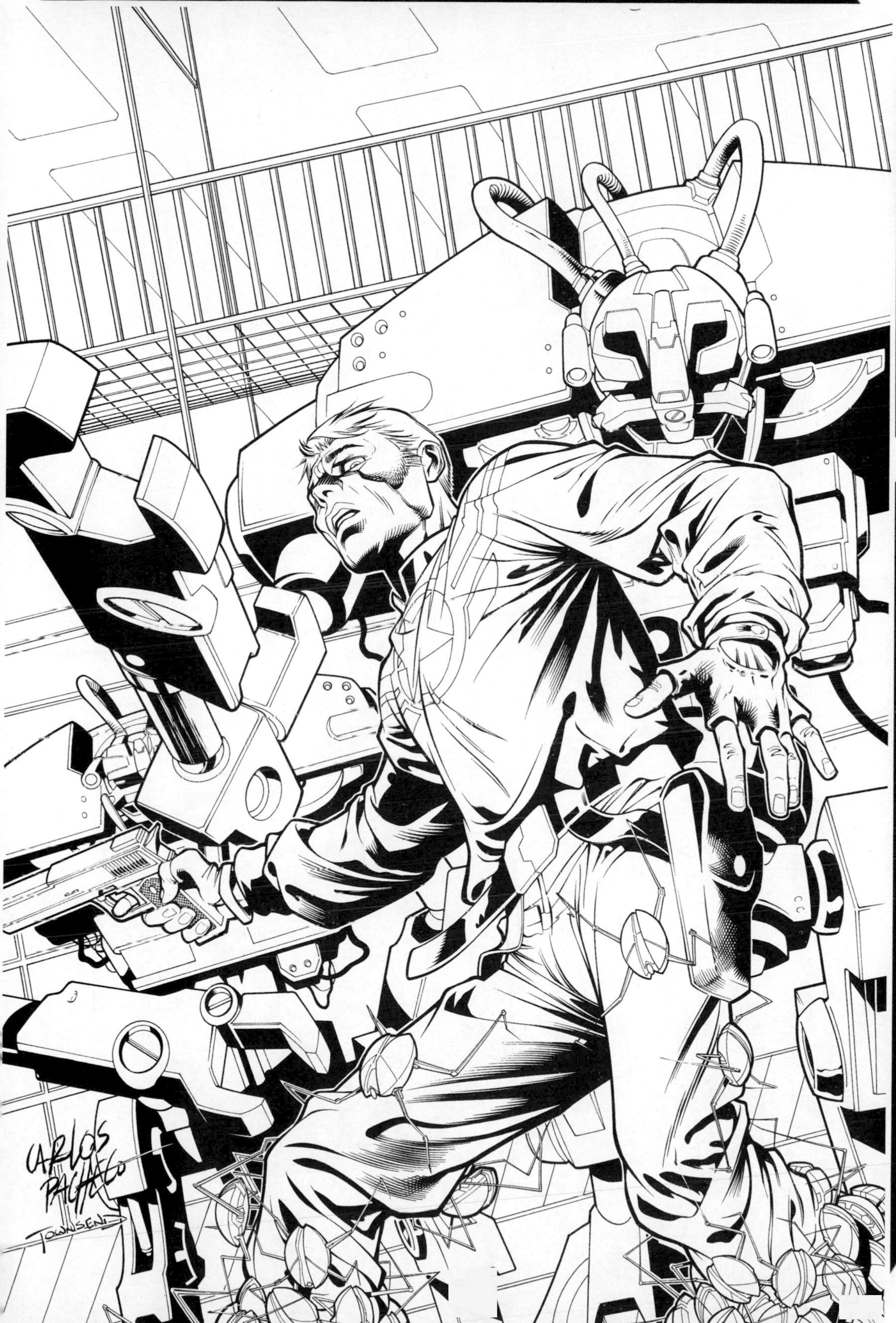
CARLOS PACHECO
TOWNSEND

#4 INKS
BY CARLOS PACHECO

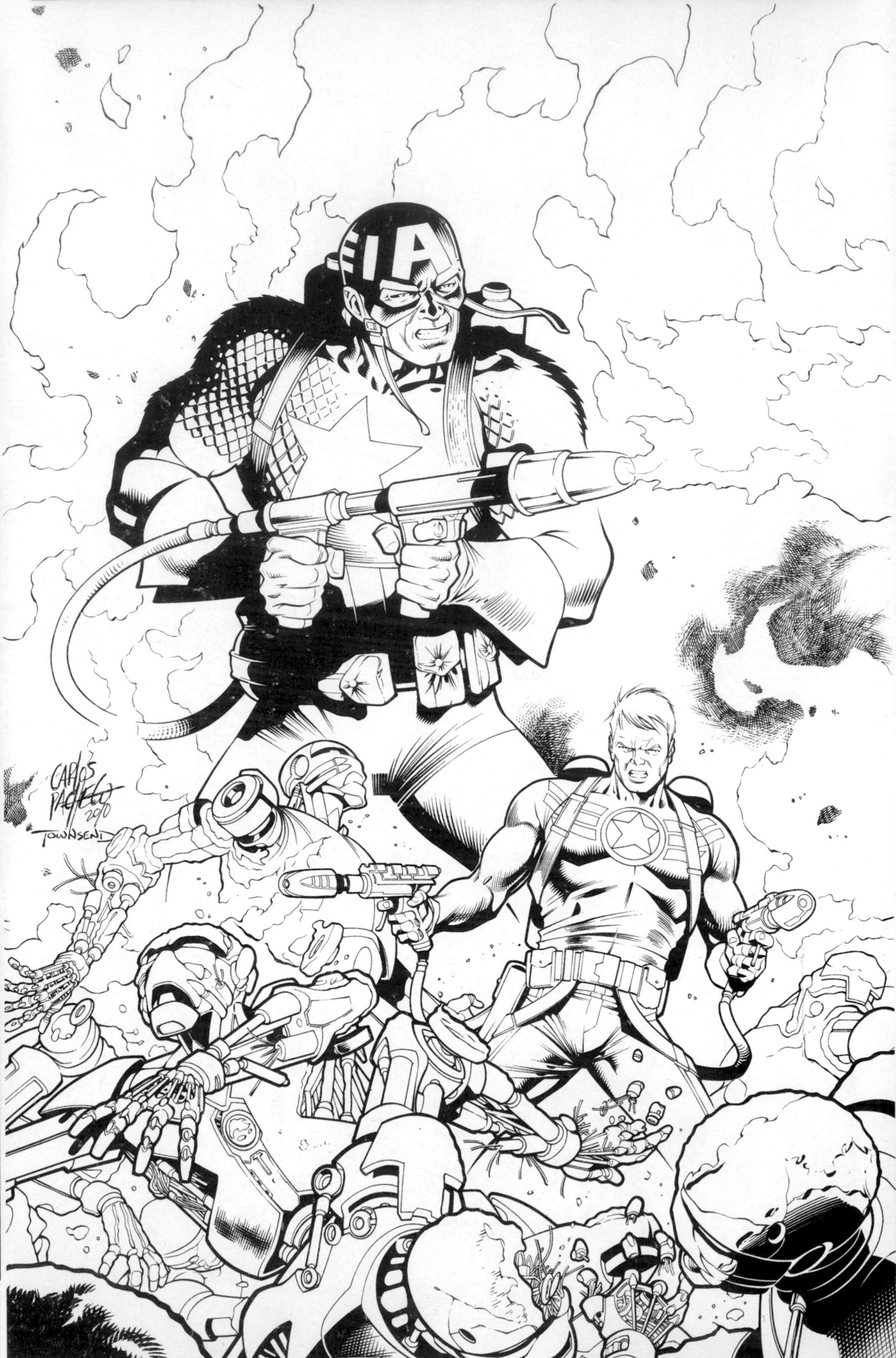
CARLOS PACHECO
TOWNSEND